AGAINST ISLAMOPHOBIA: MUSLIM COMMUNITIES, SOCIAL-EXCLUSION AND THE LISBON PROCESS IN EUROPE

AGAINST ISLAMOPHOBIA: MUSLIM COMMUNITIES, SOCIAL-EXCLUSION AND THE LISBON PROCESS IN EUROPE

ARNO TAUSCH,
CHRISTIAN BISCHOF,
TOMAZ KASTRUN
AND
KARL MUELLER

Nova Science Publishers, Inc.
New York

For permission to use material from this book please contact us:
Telephone 631-231-7269; Fax 631-231-8175
Web Site: http://www.novapublishers.com

NOTICE TO THE READER

The Publisher has taken reasonable care in the preparation of this book, but makes no expressed or implied warranty of any kind and assumes no responsibility for any errors or omissions. No liability is assumed for incidental or consequential damages in connection with or arising out of information contained in this book. The Publisher shall not be liable for any special, consequential, or exemplary damages resulting, in whole or in part, from the readers' use of, or reliance upon, this material.

Independent verification should be sought for any data, advice or recommendations contained in this book. In addition, no responsibility is assumed by the publisher for any injury and/or damage to persons or property arising from any methods, products, instructions, ideas or otherwise contained in this publication.

This publication is designed to provide accurate and authoritative information with regard to the subject matter covered herein. It is sold with the clear understanding that the Publisher is not engaged in rendering legal or any other professional services. If legal or any other expert assistance is required, the services of a competent person should be sought. FROM A DECLARATION OF PARTICIPANTS JOINTLY ADOPTED BY A COMMITTEE OF THE AMERICAN BAR ASSOCIATION AND A COMMITTEE OF PUBLISHERS.

LIBRARY OF CONGRESS CATALOGING-IN-PUBLICATION DATA

Against Islamophobia : Muslim communities, social exclusion, and the Lisbon process in Europe / Arno Tausch ... [et al.].
     p. cm.
  Includes index.
  ISBN-13: 978-1-60021-535-3 (hardcover)
  ISBN-10: 1-60021-535-1 (hardcover)
  1. Muslims--Europe. 2. Islamophobia--Europe. 3. Marginality, Social--Europe. I. Tausch, Arno, 1951-
D1056.2.M87A37 2007
305.6'97094--dc22
                              2006101094

Published by Nova Science Publishers, Inc. ✤ New York

CONTENTS

SUMMARY[1]

While there is a never-ending debate on Islamism, Islamist terrorism and the identity of Europe *vis-à-vis* growing Muslim communities in Europe, there are hardly any solid cross-national data being presented on the real extent of the Islamist threat facing Europe, and on the social conditions that lead to Islamist radicalism. By and large, our *rigorous quantitative results*, based on the first systematic use of the Muslim community data contained in the *"European Social Survey"* (ESS) all support a socio-liberal view of "migration" and "integration", compatible with much of the rest of current European political economic thinking regarding the future alternatives for the European Union, and contradict the very extended current alarmist political discourse in Western Europe.

First we show with new data that the much hailed *"European social model"* is a myth, when you compare poverty rates in OECD countries and in Europe on the basis of absolute income data, and not just poverty lines in terms of national means. The more that absolute poverty grows in Western Europe, largely due to failed integration policies, and due to the fact that the European Union expands and takes in new members characterized by low average incomes and large scale poverty rates of their own, the old national and relative poverty lines (in terms of 60 % of the national median) become obsolete.

As large scale poverty of Europe's Muslim communities threatens to grow, political radicalism might fall on a fertile ground. But we present materials, based on the ESS that give strong support to the hypothesis that *passive support for Islamist radicalism in Europe and the complete distrust in democracy does not exceed 400.000 persons*. We also compare our research results with the recent PEW data. By and large, the two datasets yield the same results. Regrettable as Islamist extremism in Europe might be, it is a far way from alarmist views that present "Islam" in Europe as such as being incompatible with the future of democracy.

We also find strong evidence that *Muslim communities in Europe are not different from other religious communities in their tendency towards secularism*. We also find that Muslim economic and social alienation in Europe very much corresponds to deficiencies of the implementation of the "Lisbon" process. Using the ESS cross-national and quantitative data, we first estimate a new UNDP-type index of *"Muslim development"* in Europe, based on

- the percentage of the Muslim community living above poverty
- the percentage of the Muslim community expressing trust in democracy
- the percentage of the Muslim community expressing trust in the legal system

---

[1] The authors would like to emphasize that the original data as well as other files are all freely available from the Lalisio Scientific Network in Germany at *http://www.lalisio.info/lalisio/members/m_TAUSCH/publications /114986208075/114986228444/*

- the percentage of the Muslim community expressing trust in parliament
- the percentage of the Muslim community expressing trust in the police

Likewise, we construct another UNDP type index, which we call *"Muslim empowerment index"*, which measures

- a small difference in the percentage of the non-Muslim communities and the Muslim community of a European country living above poverty
- a small difference in the percentage of the non-Muslim communities and the Muslim community of a European country expressing trust in democracy
- a small difference in the percentage of the non-Muslim communities and the Muslim community of a European country expressing trust in the legal system
- a small difference in the percentage of the non-Muslim communities and the Muslim community of a European country expressing trust in parliament
- a small difference in the percentage of the non-Muslim communities and the Muslim community of a European country expressing trust in the police

Also, indices of growth over time between the ESS surveys 2002 and 2004 for these two basic indices are being constructed. *Indicator performance closely correlates with a combined European Union Lisbon strategy index*, which was already presented elsewhere in the literature (Tausch, 2006; Tausch and Heshmati, 2006). The performances of the ESS countries are also compared with indicators of economic growth and gender empowerment, and ESS data are used to construct also a Muslim Human Development Index for several European countries.

Keywords: Index numbers, labor discrimination, economic integration, economic development – general, comparative studies of countries.

Chapter 1

INTRODUCTION

The author of this essay shares the analysis by the US-American diplomat Timothy M. Savage, according to whom European decision makers completely failed to address the social distress of large sections of the more than 5% (2050 predictably 20%) of the European population, constituted by the Muslims in Western Europe. However, the basic message of the present publication is that a forward looking policy that adheres to the goals of the Lisbon process with its requirements for a social coherence oriented policy will be able to address the basic issues of integration.

Needless to say here that large scale and even growing poverty of the Muslim population in Europe would squarely contradict the main principles of the "Lisbon process" that aims to increment economic growth to 3 percent a year, to increase employment and combat unemployment, to reduce social exclusion and poverty, and to improve the environment (Tausch, 2006; Tausch and Heshmati, 2006). As it is also well known, the 14 main structural "Lisbon" agenda indicators, created to measure progress in meeting the Lisbon targets, play an important role in European policy making. The Lisbon lists of indicators, apart from the debt-related well-known Maastricht criteria of the European Monetary Union, are perhaps the most important checklists for government success or failure in Europe today. They are omnipresent in the public political as well as in the scientific debate and are defined as:

1. GDP per capita in PPS
2. Labor productivity
3. Employment rate
4. Employment rate of older workers
5. Educational attainment (20-24)
6. Research and Development expenditure
7. Comparative „price levels" (developed on the basis of the relationship between gross domestic product at exchange rates and gross domestic products at purchasing power parity rates (the Commission maintaining that a low value is good result))
8. Business investment
9. At risk-of-poverty rate (low value good result)
10. Long-term unemployment rate (low value good result)
11. Dispersion of regional employment rates (low value good result)
12. Greenhouse gas emissions (low value good result)
13. Energy intensity of the economy (low value good result)

14. Volume of freight transport (low value good result)

Large scale failure to properly integrate the European Muslim population would mean failure of the Lisbon targets 3, 4, 5, 9, 10, and 11 and would negatively affect targets 1 and 2, and most probably target 8 as well.

Needless to say that Europe will be confronted in the coming years by an increasing phenomenon of Muslim migration, with which the aging continent has to come to terms with. The picture about population potentials in contiguous surrounding territories is clear indeed:

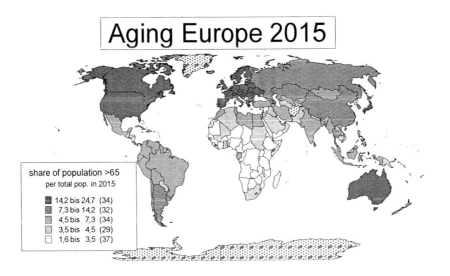

Map 1. the aging continent and its neighbors.

Source: our own calculations from UNDP, 2003 – 2006. "Bis" is shorthand for: ranging from … to

In this publication, we systematically use data gathered by European Social Survey Project, financed by the European Commission, to construct for the first time in the literature really comparable indicators of the social exclusion of Muslims in the enlarged European Union.

Needless to say that such an evaluation touches upon almost every major decision pending in the Union – the enlargement process, Turkey, what to do next with migration especially from North Africa and the Middle East, the rifts that appear in the social systems of major European Union countries, etc.

Chapter 2

THE MYTH OF THE EUROPEAN SOCIAL MODEL AND THE THREE MAJOR POVERTY GROUPS IN THE EXPANDED EU-25: MUSLIMS IN THE WEST, AND PEOPLE IN STRUCTURAL UNEMPLOYMENT REGIONS AND THE ROMA COMMUNITIES IN THE EAST

There is reason to believe – as we will explain below – that the growing signs of crisis of the "European social model" cannot be any longer disconnected from the social marginalization and the poverty of the 15 million or more Muslims, living in the countries of the European Union. Thus we start our evidence with a very thorough re-analysis of existing comparative poverty data in the framework of the "Lisbon process".

The official discourse on the "European social model" is characterized for years by a jargon like this. Such recent texts might be encountered at random:

Source: European Parliament
Published Friday, 8 September, 2006 - 06:11
http://www.egovmonitor.com/node/7511

The European Social Model "reflects a common set of values, based on the preservation of peace, social justice, equality, solidarity, the promotion of freedom and democracy and respect of human rights". According to MEPs, "in the last 60 years this set of common values has allowed a growing EU to successfully become an area of greater economic prosperity and social justice". They underline that social policies, when appropriately designed "cannot be regarded as a cost but, instead, as a positive factor in the EU's economic growth". Although Member States have different social systems, and have implemented these values in different ways, they commonly aim to attain a balance between economic growth and social solidarity, and this is reflected in the European Social Model as a unity of values with a diversity of systems, members underline. (...) MEPs stress the necessity to preserve and enhance the values associated with the European Social Model and the high social standards already achieved. They are convinced that the economic and social systems must be urgently reformed where they fail to meet the criteria of efficiency and socially sustainable development, and where they are inadequate to tackle the challenges of demographic change, globalisation and the IT revolution.. Also to restore citizen's confidence in the EU project, which provides jobs, growth and prosperity, the EU's commitment to a Social Europe needs to be renewed, members stress.

(...) Members underline that even if employment and social policy remain broadly within national competence, the EU needs to create an economic and social framework which allows Member States to implement reforms as necessary at national level, according to their own economic, social and political circumstances. They call on the Commission and the Council to respect the initial equilateral triangle of the Lisbon Strategy and to develop an approach that is better balanced between economic coordination on the one hand and employment and social protection policy on the other. The Commission is asked to take further initiatives to achieve full implementation of the internal market, having regard to exclude any race to the bottom in social, consumer or environmental standards. The Commission shall also incorporate already now the social dimension in its impact analyses, in accordance with the social clause provided for in the proposed Constitutional Treaty.

Members recognise the advantages of 'flexicurity' systems which Member States should adopt. They consider them as a means of promoting reconciliation of work-life balance and work and life-cycle concepts. Since many Member States are far from achieving the Lisbon Strategy objectives they are called to achieve, in particular, the specific targets set for employment, especially of women and young people, Research and Development investment, child care and lifelong learning. Member States shall furthermore undertake reforms in order to ensure the financial sustainability of national social systems, without prejudicing acquired rights, mutual support and intergenerational solidarity. They should also improve the coordination of their tax policies with a view to avoiding harmful tax competition, ensuring sustainable financing for social protection and making tax policy more employment friendly. The EU funds, such as the European Structural Funds, shall be used more efficiently to co-finance national reforms. MEPs underline that any successful reform of the social systems should involve all stakeholders, in particular the social partners and civil society.

While there has been large emphasis in recent social policy literature on different aspects of social exclusion and relative poverty in Europe and the Lisbon process, *four basic tendencies* so far have not been adequately addressed. These issues make the comparative research about European poverty and the social groups, constituting the European poor, all the more important:

1) the realization that – as the Union expands – our social situation more and more becomes comparable to that of other continents. There seems to be a definitive *end of a specific "European social model".* Large scale Muslim poverty in Western Europe, Roma poverty in Eastern Europe and the necessity to cut back on the pension entitlements of Europe's growing elderly population all contribute to the fact that today, there are 8.7 per cent of the population in the United States who receive 40 % of the United States median equivalized household income, while in key EU states this percentage is already higher than the corresponding US figure. *In France, the UK, Ireland and Italy is already higher than in the US,* while in Germany, Belgium, Denmark, the Netherlands,

and Sweden this percentage is only somewhat lower than in the US (8.7 percent versus 7 percent to 7.9 percent in these key West European states).

2) *poverty risk,* i.e. the measure that indicates to us how many times a *certain social group* is likely to fall into the poverty trap, more and more becomes a question whether or not a European resident is a citizen of his country or she or he is **a** *"foreigner" from outside the borders of the EU-25.* Calculations on this phenomenon only slowly become available, but the data already at the disposal of social science are very clear and suggest that on the level of the old Western European EU-15, the poverty risk for foreigners is two times higher than for EU-citizens. We also compared the poverty risk of foreigners in the EU with the poverty risk of being under age 20, above age 60, of living in a household with three or more children, a single parent household, or of being unemployed. In *"old Europe"*, foreigners were confronted with the highest risk of being poor in Austria, Belgium, Finland, France, the Netherlands, Portugal, and Spain and at the level of the entire EU-15 countries (or rather 14, because data for Sweden were missing for this comparison) in the late 1990s. These data were based on European Community Household (ECHP) data evaluations; forthcoming new calculations by Eurostat, based on the new EU-SILC data system, will most probably become available by the beginning of 2007[1].

3) First calculations published by the European Foundation for the Improvement of Living and Working Conditions (Fahey, 2005) dramatically emphasize *the consequences of the high levels of absolute poverty in the new Europe of 25 countries.* Assuming that absolute US poverty today is not too far away from the British figures, we can only gather that the absolute poverty rates of marginal groups – and hundreds of thousands of Muslims among them – in Europe are really very high (see graphs 1a and 1c).

4) Add to this the millions of poor unemployed people in Eastern Europe and the millions of destitute Roma and Sinti in Eastern and Southeastern Europe, and you can imagine that *poverty in the US and the EU-25 is today really comparable or even surpasses it.* The overall performance of the European region in terms of the development of the UNDP human development index, which is a very sensitive measure to grasp inter-temporal changes in social conditions, is unsatisfactory, especially in countries with a large Muslim community, i.e. the social conditions of hundreds of thousands of Muslims in Europe seem to have stagnated or even deteriorated over the last years (see map 2 and appendix 6). Apart from that, European poverty statistics, based on the traditional criterion of poverty as defined in terms of the percentage of population falling under 60 % of the national median income, are extremely biased and do not grasp the true amount of poverty in the EU-25 (Graph 1c, Table 1d and 1e):

Thus, our combined evidence, which all implies the enormous and growing social policy task of alleviating Muslim poverty in Western Europe, and Roma and structural employment poverty in Eastern Europe, suggests the following:

---

[1] Personal communication from Dr. Ian Dennis, Eurostat, Luxembourg

- Absolute poverty rates in several European states are higher than in the US in terms of the threshold – 40 % or lower than the purchasing power of the US median
- New calculations made available in this publication even suggest that poverty rates in terms of a new measure, developed by Professor Toney Fahey, based on a EU-25 wide threshold of 60 % or less than the median income in the entire EU-25, are very high in the new member countries of the Union, and exceed 10 % in the West European countries UK, Spain, Germany, Greece, and Portugal. The German poverty rate of 25.5 % is especially distressing, considering the demographic, economic and political importance of Germany in the wider European Union
- Survival rates at age 65 in many European Union member countries by far are below the respective values for Japan, Switzerland, Australia, New Zealand and Canada and – in some countries of Eastern Europe – even in the US, with huge gender gaps of more than 5 years between low male and higher female survival rates being encountered in most EU-25 nations
- Human development growth is more and more stagnating in Western Europe, and Western Europe is losing it's once very high world ranks on the UNDP human development scale
- Poverty rates for migrants and non-EU-citizens that are 1.5, two or even three times higher than the national average were to be encountered in Germany, the Netherlands, Belgium, Luxembourg, France, Spain, Portugal, Austria, and Finland. With the exception of Finland, all these cases have to be analyzed in the context of their large Muslim communities
- Combined poverty indicators (see below) seem to suggest the same diagnosis, for which Spain, the UK, Greece, the Slovak Republic, Hungary, Ireland, Italy, Poland and Portugal all had to be ranked below the US. With the exception of the Irish Republic, all other cases can be well explained by the factors: Muslim and immigrant poverty; structural unemployment in backward and old industrial regions, or Roma and Sinti communities
- An analysis of key UNDP indicators (Table 1d) reveals that the worst performers in the EU-25 in terms of human development are easily being outperformed by Latin American countries for 8 of the 9 indicators used, and by Arab Mediterranean countries for 5 of the 9 indicators used.
- Even worse, the European Commission and the member states absolutely did not as yet answer this crisis by using adequate statistical instruments. Instead of using the framework of the United Nations statistical system, Eurostat analyzes poverty in terms of the famous 60 % or less of the national median income criterion, which of course becomes the more biased, the lower the level of development of a nation becomes. Our statistical analysis, based on the data of Professor Tony Fahey, suggests that in comparison to the necessary EU-25-wide median income, poverty rates in the new member countries in the Baltic's and in Bulgaria and Romania as well as in the candidate country Turkey are being underestimated by a factor of 40 % or more.

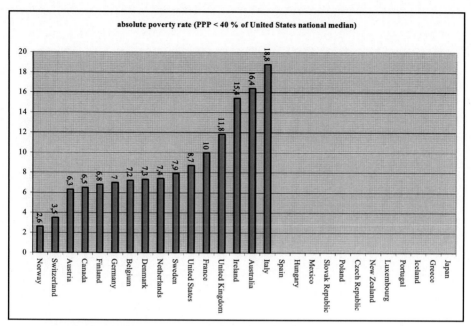

Source: our own calculations from Schmitt J. and Zipperer B. (2006).
Graph 1a. absolute poverty in OECD countries.

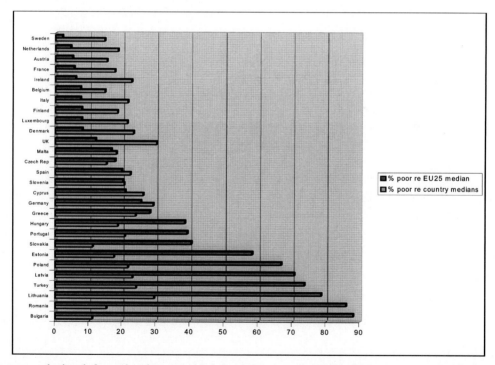

Source: calculated from the data provided by Fahey et al. (2005) (European Foundation for the Improvement of Living and Working Conditions). Professor Fahey's results are the first published comparison of European poverty rates after enlargement with the EU-25 wide median income as the poverty level. The original EXCEL-spreadsheet was kindly put at our disposal by Professor Fahey.

Graph 1b. absolute household poverty in Europe – EQLS data, on the basis of an EU-25 wide median income

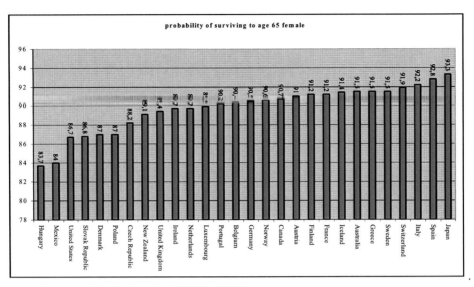

Source: graph, arranged with data from UNDP (2005).
Graph 1c. the human development dimension of poverty in OECD countries – female survival rates.

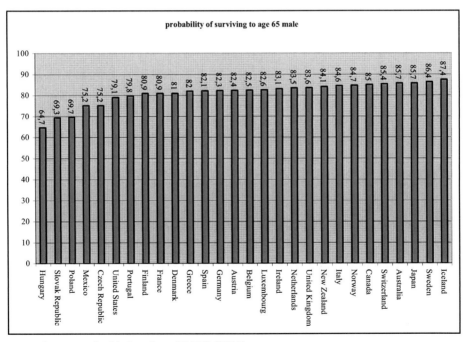

Source: graph, arranged with data from UNDP (2005).
Graph 1d. the human development dimension of poverty in OECD countries – male survival rates.

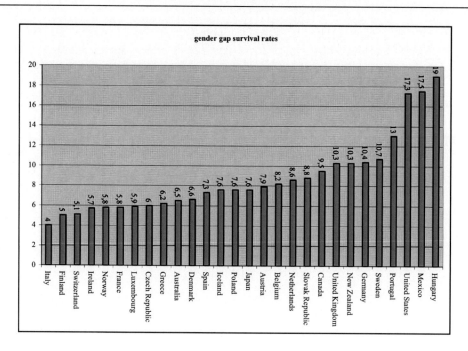

Source: our own calculations from UNDP (2006).
Graph 1d. the human development dimension of poverty in OECD countries –gender gaps in survival rates.

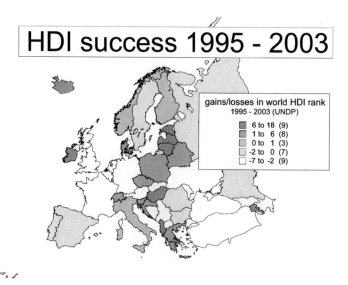

Legend: Dark shades indicate a good performance. Changes in world human development ranks, 1995 – 2003. Data source: UNDP, 2005.
Map 2. gains in human development world ranks in Europe, 1995 – 2003.

To evaluate European poverty indicators at once, we constructed a UNDP-type combined "avoidance of poverty indicator" (Table 1b) from the data of Table 1a, which summarizes available UNDP, CEPR and Eurostat materials on the subject.

The UNDP type indicators are based on a simple principle, designed in the 1990s by Nobel laureate Amartya Sen: if you want to combine 2 or more variables to an indicator, calculate for each of the variables a dimension index, using the formula (UNDP, 2005):

(1) Dimension index = (actual value – minimum value) / (maximum value – minimum value)

Calculating the famous *"Human Development Index"* of the United Nations Human Development Programme, one is supposed to proceed in the following way. According to forumula (1), one first has to calculate a *life expectancy component*, called *"life expectancy index"*. Then, the same formula is used for an *"education index"*, based on the figures for adult literacy and gross enrollment (the weight for adult literacy is 2/3, and 1/3 for gross enrollment). The *"GDP index"* is now based on a small alteration of formula (1), working with the log GDP. In earlier years, the UNDP worked exactly with formula (1). Today, the UNDP calculates according to the following formula:

(1a) *GDP index* = (log (actual value GDP PPP per capita) minus log (100))/(log (maximum value GDP PPP per capita) minus log (100))

The UNDP HDI then will be the combined result of

(2) Human development index = 1/3 * (life expectancy index) + 1/3 * (education index) + 1/3 * (GDP index)

In our case, we calculated, using formula (1) the 8 different dimension indices for our new *avoidance of poverty index:*

- probability of surviving to age 65 female
- probability of surviving to age 65 male
- relative poverty rate (PPP < 40 % of national median)
- absolute poverty rate (PPP < 40 % of United States national median)
- relative poverty rate (PPP < 60 % of national median, mid 1990s)
- relative poverty rate (PPP < 60 % of national median, mid 2000s, Eurostat)
- % of the population aged 24-64 with at least upper secondary education
- quintile ratio (difference in incomes between the richest 20 % and the poorest 20 %.

Due to missing values, we were satisfied with simply calculating the means from the 8 available different components:

- (3) avoidance of poverty index = the means from

- component index probability of surviving to age 65 female - component index probability of surviving to age 65 male - component index avoiding a high relative poverty rate (PPP < 40 % of national median) - component index avoiding a high absolute poverty rate (PPP < 40 % of United States national median) - component index avoiding a high relative poverty rate (PPP < 60 % of national median, mid 1990s)

- component index avoiding a high relative poverty rate (PPP < 60 % of national median, mid 2000s, Eurostat)
- component index % of the population aged 24-64 with at least upper secondary education
- component index avoiding a high quintile ratio

Admittedly, the data used here are provisional and deficient. But today, *Japan* outperforms most probably even the very advanced European countries Norway, Sweden, Switzerland, Finland, Iceland, Austria, Czech Republic, while *New Zealand* and *Canada* outperform Denmark, the Netherlands, Germany, Belgium, France and Luxembourg, and the *United States and Australia* are ranked ahead of Spain, the United Kingdom, Greece, the Slovak Republic, Hungary, Ireland, Italy, Poland and Portugal.

Only Mexico presents an overall more dramatic poverty picture than all the combined European Union countries (Tables 1a to 1d). Especially the comparative data from Table 1d reveal how the *"European social model"* has become a myth under the pressures of globalization:

As we already stated, the cast-like character of European society and the discrimination patterns that we often encounter, emerge from the thorough statistical analysis of poverty risk rates in Europe. Many years ago, Mancur Olson (Olson, 1982) analyzed such social discrimination patterns and came to the conclusion that racial and ethnic discrimination are incompatible with the workings of a liberal market economy:

The dire consequences of such discrimination patterns are the "Latin Americanization" and the "Mediterraneanization" of the European Union.

Table 1a. social exclusion in Europe by international comparison – the raw data

	Proba-bility of surviving to age 65 female	Proba-bility of surviving to age 65 male	relative poverty rate (PPP < 40 % of national median)	absolute poverty rate (PPP < 40 % of United States national median)	relative poverty rate (PPP < 60 % of national median, mid 1990s)	relative poverty rate (PPP < 60 % of national median, mid 2000s, Eurostat)	% of the population aged 24-64 with at least upper secondary education	quintile ratio
Australia	91,5	85,7	6,6	16,4	18,8		62,0	7,0
Austria	91,0	82,4	4,0	6,3	13,7	13,0	79,0	4,7
Belgium	90,4	82,5	3,2	7,2	13,2	15,0	62,0	4,5
Canada	90,7	85,0	6,5	6,5	16,5		84,0	5,8
Czech Republic	88,2	75,2				8,0	86,0	3,5
Denmark	87,0	81,0	4,9	7,3	12,0	11,0	81,0	4,3
Finland	91,2	80,9	2,1	6,8	10,8	11,0	76,0	3,8
France	91,2	80,9	3,3	10,0	13,5	14,0	65,0	5,6
Germany	90,5	82,3	4,2	7,0	15,7	16,0	83,0	4,3
Greece	91,5	82,0			21,7	20,0	51,0	6,2

Table 1a. Continued

	Probability of surviving to age 65 female	Probability of surviving to age 65 male	relative poverty rate (PPP < 40 % of national median)	absolute poverty rate (PPP < 40 % of United States national median)	relative poverty rate (PPP < 60 % of national median, mid 1990s)	relative poverty rate (PPP < 60 % of national median, mid 2000s, Eurostat)	% of the population aged 24-64 with at least upper secondary education	quintile ratio
Hungary	83,7	64,7				12,0	74,0	3,8
Iceland	91,4	87,4				10,0	59,0	
Ireland	89,7	83,1	8,0	15,4	20,7	21,0	62,0	6,1
Italy	92,2	84,6	7,3	18,8	21,9	19,0	44,0	6,5
Japan	93,3	85,7			13,9		84,0	3,4
Luxembourg	89,9	82,6				11,0	59,0	
Mexico	84,0	75,2			27,7		21,0	19,3
Netherlands	89,7	83,5	4,5	7,4	13,5	12,0	66,0	5,1
New Zealand	89,1	84,1					78,0	6,8
Norway	90,6	84,7	2,8	2,6	14,6	11,0	87,0	3,9
Poland	87,0	69,7				17,0	48,0	5,5
Portugal	90,2	79,8				21,0	23,0	8,0
Slovak Republic	86,8	69,3				21,0	87,0	4,0
Spain	92,8	82,1	5,2			20,0	43,0	5,4
Sweden	91,5	86,4	3,6	7,9	10,3	11,0	82,0	4,0
Switzerland	91,9	85,4	4,0	3,5	11,8		70,0	5,8
United Kingdom	89,4	83,6	5,4	11,8	19,5	18,0	65,0	7,2
United States	86,7	79,1	10,7	8,7	24,0		88,0	8,4

Source: our own calculations from UNDP HDR 2005; CEPR, Eurostat.

Table 1b. towards an overall UNDP type indicator of poverty avoidance in Europe, based on the materials of Table 1a

	component index probability of surviving to age 65 female	Component index probability of surviving to age 65 male	Component index relative poverty rate (PPP < 40 % of national median)	component index absolute poverty rate (PPP < 40 % of United States national median)	component index relative poverty rate (PPP < 60 % of national median, mid 1990s)	component index relative poverty rate (PPP < 60 % of national median, mid 2000s, Eurostat)	component index % of the population aged 24-64 with at least upper secondary education	Component index quintile ratio	Avoidance of poverty index
Japan	1,000	0,925			0,793		0,940	1,000	0,932
Norway	0,719	0,881	0,919	1,000	0,753	0,769	0,985	0,969	0,874
Sweden	0,813	0,956	0,826	0,673	1,000	0,769	0,910	0,962	0,864
Switzerland	0,854	0,912	0,779	0,944	0,914		0,731	0,849	0,855
Finland	0,781	0,714	1,000	0,741	0,971	0,769	0,821	0,975	0,846
Iceland	0,802	1,000				0,846	0,567		0,804
Austria	0,760	0,780	0,779	0,772	0,805	0,615	0,866	0,918	0,787
Czech Republic	0,469	0,463				1,000	0,970	0,994	0,779
New Zealand	0,562	0,855					0,851	0,786	0,764
Canada	0,729	0,894	0,488	0,759	0,644		0,940	0,849	0,758
Denmark	0,344	0,718	0,674	0,710	0,902	0,769	0,896	0,943	0,745
Netherlands	0,625	0,828	0,721	0,704	0,816	0,692	0,672	0,893	0,744
Germany	0,708	0,775	0,756	0,728	0,690	0,385	0,925	0,943	0,739
Belgium	0,698	0,784	0,872	0,716	0,833	0,462	0,612	0,931	0,738
France	0,781	0,714	0,860	0,543	0,816	0,538	0,657	0,862	0,721
Luxembourg	0,646	0,789				0,769	0,567		0,693
United States	0,313	0,634	0,000	0,623	0,213	1,615	1,000	0,686	0,635
Australia	0,813	0,925	0,477	0,148	0,511		0,612	0,774	0,609
Spain	0,948	0,767	0,640			0,077	0,328	0,874	0,606
United Kingdom	0,594	0,833	0,616	0,432	0,471	0,231	0,657	0,761	0,574
Greece	0,813	0,762			0,345	0,077	0,448	0,824	0,545
Slovak Republic	0,323	0,203				0,000	0,985	0,962	0,495
Hungary	0,000	0,000				0,692	0,791	0,975	0,492
Ireland	0,625	0,811	0,314	0,210	0,402	0,000	0,612	0,830	0,475
Italy	0,885	0,877	0,395	0,000	0,333	0,154	0,343	0,805	0,474
Poland	0,344	0,220				0,308	0,403	0,868	0,429
Portugal	0,677	0,665				0,000	0,030	0,711	0,417
Mexico	0,031	0,463			0,000		0,000	0,000	0,099

The countries printed in indented letters are not members of the European Union.

Table 1c. the poverty risk rates of different social groups in Europe – 1990s

relative poverty risk for the different social groups	Germany	Denmark	Netherland	Belgium	Luxembourg	France	UK	Ireland	Italy	Greece	Spain	Portugal	Austria	Finland	EU-14
gender male	92	93	94	93	98	94	90	93	96	98	100	93	87	96	94
gender female	107	107	105	106	102	105	109	107	104	102	100	106	112	104	106
age < 20	127	48	127	118	146	121	128	131	123	92	128	103	110	73	122
age 20 - 29	123	182	171	90	84	123	99	69	128	95	95	64	87	173	114
age 30 - 49	87	53	77	80	81	74	71	90	84	72	96	78	83	79	81
age 50 - 59	79	73	59	88	109	83	65	76	97	94	90	95	73	100	82
age 60 +	93	195	77	118	79	105	126	93	82	147	84	153	125	122	104
single parent hh	227	67	243	150	147	175	224	154	108	108	111	126	142	98	177
couple with 3 or more children	131	40	138	118	183	104	125	134	173	92	188	189	224	38	129
low education	104	148	127	137	110	135	123	115	113	145	114	111	135	139	122
EU citizens	89	103	90	93	86	90	87	82	97	103	95	98	86	108	92
non-EU citizens	177	128	319	204	171	313	101	113	72	128	232	192	254	396	203
unemployed	171	82	192	179	182	197	200	164	212	134	153	89	157	203	180
pensioners	93	189	162	109	98	99	128	68	66	150	68	143	142	118	99
inactive	135	188	123	140	120	162	161	130	132	108	115	131	147	202	138
total	100	100	100	100	100	100	100	100	100	100	100	100	100	100	100

Source: our own compilations from BMSG Sozialbericht 2001.

Table 1d. Social cohesion in the EU-25, in Latin America and the Caribbean, and in the MEDA partner countries of the European Union

Criterion	Which Latin American and Caribbean countries outperform worst performing EU nation?	Which Arab MEDA EU-partner countries outperform worst performing EU nation?	Worst EU-25 nation	Value for worst EU-25 nation	Value for the US
human development index	Barbados, Argentina, Chile, Uruguay, Costa Rica		Latvia	0, 836	0, 944
inequality between richest 20 % and poorest 20 %	Jamaica	Egypt, Jordan, Algeria, Morocco, Tunisia	Portugal	8	8, 4
life expectancy at birth	Costa Rica, Chile, Cuba, Dominica, Uruguay, Mexico, Barbados, Panama, Argentina, Ecuador, Antigua and Barbuda, Venezuela, Colombia, Saint Lucia, Belize	Libya, Tunisia, Syria, Lebanon	Latvia	71, 6	77, 4
probability at birth of surviving to age 65, female	Chile, Costa Rica, Cuba, Uruguay, Panama, Argentina, Mexico, Venezuela, Ecuador	Tunisia, Syria, Libya	Latvia	81, 9	86, 7
probability at birth of surviving to age 65, male	Costa Rica, Cuba, Chile, Panama, Mexico, Barbados, Uruguay, Ecuador, Argentina, Venezuela, Belize, Saint Lucia, Paraguay, Colombia, Saint Vincent, Peru, Jamaica, El Salvador, Nicaragua, Trinidad and Tobago, Honduras, Suriname, Brazil, Bahamas, Dominican Republic, Bolivia, Guatemala	Syria, Tunisia, Algeria, Lebanon, Jordan, Morocco, Egypt	Estonia	57, 2	79, 1
ratio of estimated female to male earned income	Jamaica, Bahamas, Barbados, Uruguay, Panama, Colombia, Trinidad and Tobago, Nicaragua, Bolivia, El Salvador, Brazil, Venezuela, Guyana, Chile, Mexico, Honduras, Costa Rica, Argentina, Dominican Republic	Morocco, Tunisia	Austria	0, 35	0, 62
real income of the poorest 20 % in purchasing power parities	none		Latvia	3749	10142

Table 1d. (Continued)

criterion	Which Latin American and Caribbean countries outperform worst performing EU nation?	Which Arab MEDA EU-partner countries outperform worst performing EU nation?	worst EU-25 nation	value for worst EU-25 nation	value for the US
gender development index	Barbados, Argentina, Chile, Uruguay		Latvia	0, 834	0, 942
gender empowerment measure	Bahamas, Costa Rica, Argentina, Trinidad and Tobago, Barbados, Mexico, Panama, Dominican Republic, Bolivia, Peru, Uruguay, Colombia, Ecuador		Malta	0, 486	0, 793

Source: Tausch (2007)

As we already mentioned, the statistical instruments used by Eurostat are not adequate any more to fully grasp this crisis, constituted by large scale Muslim poverty in the West, structural unemployment and Roma poverty in the East. Eurostat "official" poverty rates not only show with lower incomes a growing bias, but they also imply a "perverse" correlation between hard-core poverty indicators and their poverty rates. With increasing poverty (Eurostat definition, based on the national median incomes) you get rising life expectancy rates and a rising UNDP Human Development Index, while the new data set, provided by Professor Toney Fahey, seems to suggest that the EU-25-wide 60 % median income poverty criterion has 4/5 of variance in common with life expectancy and the human development index, and the relationship is indeed in the expected direction.

Table 1e. Poverty in the EU-25 according to the new criterion: poverty = below 60 % of the EU-25 wide median income

	% poor re country median	% poor re EU25 median	implicit measurement bias [over- or underestimation of poverty in % of the total population]
Bulgaria	10,9	88	-77,1
Romania	15,2	85,9	-70,7
Lithuania	29,4	78,5	-49,1
Turkey	24	73,5	-49,5
Latvia	22,9	70,5	-47,6
Poland	21,6	66,6	-45
Estonia	17,5	58,1	-40,6
Slovakia	11	40,3	-29,3
Portugal	20,7	39,1	-18,4
Hungary	18,6	38,4	-19,8
Greece	23,8	28,2	-4,4
Germany	29,1	25,5	3,6
Cyprus	26,1	20,8	5,3
Slovenia	20,5	20,2	0,3
Spain	22,3	19,8	2,5

Czech Rep	15,2	17,8	-2,6
Malta	18,2	16,7	1,5
UK	30,1	11,9	18,2
Denmark	23,2	7,9	15,3
Luxembourg	21,4	7,7	13,7
Finland	18,5	7,7	10,8
Italy	21,5	7,3	14,2
Belgium	14,7	7,3	7,4
Ireland	22,6	5,9	16,7
France	17,7	5,4	12,3
Austria	15,3	5	10,3
Netherlands	18,6	4,4	14,2
Sweden	14,6	2	12,6

Source: calculated from the data provided by Fahey et al. (2005) (European Foundation for the Improvement of Living and Working Conditions). Professor Fahey's results are the first published comparison of European poverty rates after enlargement with the EU-25 wide median income as the poverty level. The original EXCEL-spreadsheet was kindly put at our disposal by Professor Fahey.

Our graphical presentation of the measurement bias is as follows:

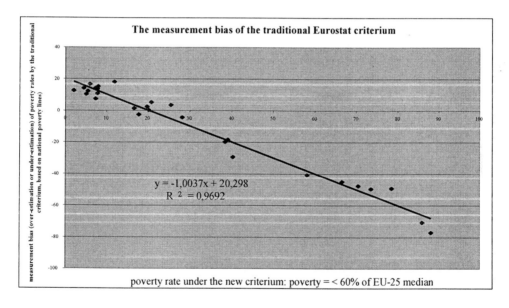

Source: calculated from the data provided by Fahey et al. (2005) (European Foundation for the Improvement of Living and Working Conditions). Professor Fahey's results are the first published comparison of European poverty rates after enlargement with the EU-25 wide median income as the poverty level. The original EXCEL-spreadsheet was kindly put at our disposal by Professor Fahey.

Graph 1e. The traditional Eurostat poverty statistics are biased.

The mentioned correlations between the old and the new poverty measures (based on national means versus the new EU-25 criterion) and UNDP life expectancy and human development indices are staggering indeed. The old national median Eurostat measure does not explain to us more than 95 % of these two hard core UNDP poverty measures, and the direction of the assumed relationship is even perverse (with more poverty you get better living conditions), while Professor Fahey's new measure receives a forceful statistical confirmation:

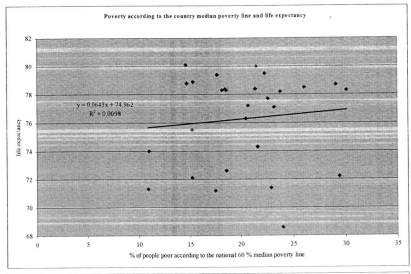

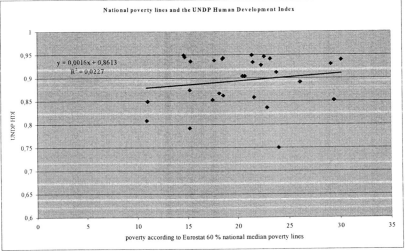

Source: calculated from the data provided by Fahey et al. (2005) (European Foundation for the Improvement of Living and Working Conditions) and UNDP, 2005. Professor Fahey's results are the first published comparison of European poverty rates after enlargement with the EU-25 wide median income as the poverty level. The original EXCEL-spreadsheet was kindly put at our disposal by Professor Fahey.

Graph 1f. The traditional Eurostat poverty statistics are biased – percentage of the population poor according to the national, Eurostat poverty lines (poverty = income below 60 % of national median) and life expectancy or the human development index. The result is a perverse positive correlation between poverty and life expectancy or the human development index.

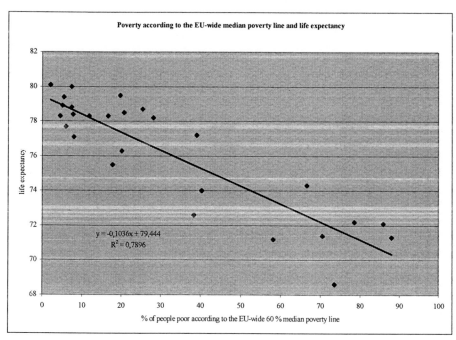

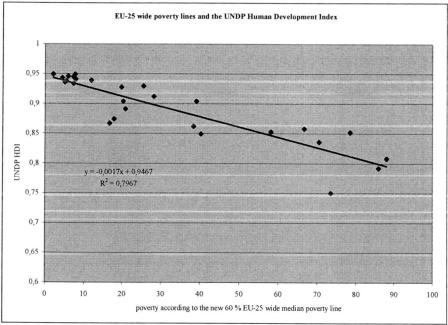

Source: calculated from the data provided by Fahey et al. (2005) (European Foundation for the Improvement of Living and Working Conditions), and UNDP, 2005. Professor Fahey's results are the first published comparison of European poverty rates after enlargement with the EU-25 wide median income as the poverty level. The original EXCEL-spreadsheet was kindly put at our disposal by Professor Fahey.

Graph 1g: The new EU-25 wide poverty statistics are NOT biased – percentage of the population poor according to the new, EU-25 wide poverty lines (poverty = income below 60 % of EU-25 median) and life expectancy or the human development index. The result is the expected negative correlation between poverty and life expectancy or the human development index.

Limited as these data may be, they seem to indicate that a more thorough, systematic study of the poverty of the more than 15 million Muslims in Europe is needed to test the hypothesis that Muslim poverty in western Europe, Roma poverty in Eastern Europe and the plight of the unemployed especially in Southern and Eastern Europe are all part of the rapid peripherization of the European continent.

At this point, we also should refer to the data compiled in the appendix to this work. Appendix 1 and 2 quotes the ESS data in more detail and mentions also the number of cases n for each country. Appendix 3 mentions the data for

- income
- trust in democracy
- trust in the legal system
- trust in parliament
- trust in the police

for the Muslim population and the non-Muslim population in Europe and in the ESS OECD reference country Israel. In the data appendix 7 – 10 to this essay, we further elaborate on the issue of proper new European poverty indices.

In appendix 7 and 8 we show that the generally unsatisfactory growth of the UNDP Human Development Index in Europe (with the exceptions of Ireland, Luxembourg, the UK, Portugal, Cyprus, Hungary, Poland, Sweden and Norway) most probably already reflects the dimensions of Muslim and Roma marginalization in Europe, especially in countries like Bulgaria, Romania, France, the Netherlands, Greece, Spain, Germany, Austria, Denmark and Italy. We calculated the residuals from a simple OLS regression, predicting the UNDP HDI (UNDP, 2005 data) in 1990 on the UNDP HDI 2003 at the level of the world system (UNDP, 2005 data). We also drew a scatter plot between the Muslim development index and these human development regression residuals. The operation shows that at least a part of the variance of the unsatisfactory human development in the 1990s and beyond in Europe (at least 1/5) can be attributed to the dimension of "Muslim discrimination". Better integrating the Muslim communities in Europe would create the conditions for an overall more satisfactory human development. Appendix 7 to 10 shows the relationships of the new EU-25 wide poverty index, developed by Professor Tony Fahey, with the UNDP Human Development Index. The UNDP HDI explains 79.67 % of the variance of the EU-25-wide 60 % median income poverty measure, and linear estimates based on the UNDP wield interesting estimates for countries within and outside the EU-25. Appendix 6 finally analyses some other interesting properties of the new index. While the country median poverty values are mainly an (insignificant) reflection of the quintile ratio, the new index is to be explained in a significant way by more than 4/5 by an insufficient human development, by a high quintile ratio, and a low international comparative price level (1/ERDI). In line with arguments put forward by the author and his associates in other publications (especially Kohler/Tausch, 2001), low comparative price levels – or as world systems theory prefers to say – unequal exchange – has a strong influence of its own on national poverty rates. We also estimate a UNDP-HDI for the European Muslim communities. French and Greek Muslims are facing a poverty that is similar to the national averages in countries like Bulgaria or Mexico.

Since dealt with structural employment and Roma poverty in Eastern Europe extensively in earlier publications (Tausch and associates, 2001 – 2007), we concentrate here on the poverty of the Muslim communities in the new enlarged Europe.

Chapter 3

METHODOLOGY OF THE EUROPEAN SOCIAL SURVEY – BASED RESULTS

The systematic analysis of *comparative* aspects of the socio-economic situation of the respective European Muslim communities, let alone the interaction of this situation with aspects of what is generally described in EU-jargon as the "Lisbon process" of catching up by 2010 with the United States of America, to make Europe the most competitive, knowledge-based economy in the world is until now absent from the literature due to lacking systematically comparable data.

Our research report, which starts from the tradition of cross-national, *quantitative* political science, economics and sociology, would like to move away the debate from the in-depth analysis of the patterns and trajectories of Muslim migration to Europe, still so common today in the literature, towards the cross-national, comparative perspective. Which policies favored "integration" and human well-being among the Muslim communities, and which policies were conspicuously absent, where were such efforts obviously less successful? Which relationships exist between the failures to integrate the some 15 million Muslim immigrants in Europe and the failures of the "Lisbon process" observable up to now?

In this report, we use the powerful instrument of the *European Social Survey* for the first time to study the situation of the Muslim communities in Europe. The ESS, financed by the European Commission, and national co-partners, is the key social scientific data collection of the EC apart from the usual Eurostat and Euro barometer data. The raw data are freely available on the internet, and can be downloaded with the advanced SPSS and SAS statistical software packages[1].

Systematic use of the ESS data up to now was made, among others, for the study of the attitudes of the majority populations in Europe towards European minorities. This study was carried out by the European Monitoring Centre on Racism and Xenophobia (EUMC) in Vienna[2]. In view of the far-reaching political debate on Islam, Islamism and Muslim communities in Europe, the deficit to use the ESS data also for the analysis of the situation of Muslims in Europe is somewhat surprising.

---

[1] *http://www.europeansocialsurvey.org/*
[2]*http://eumc.europa.eu/eumc/index.php?fuseaction=content.dsp_cat_content&catid=3fb38ad3e22bb& contentid=42369ad95426f*

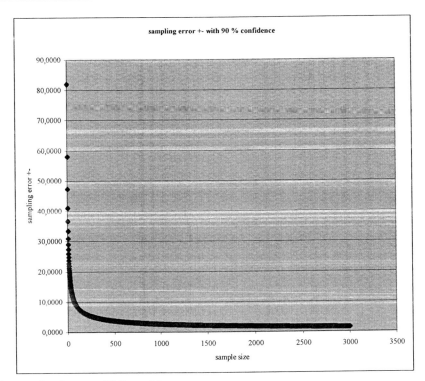

Graph 2a. margin of error at 90 % confidence.

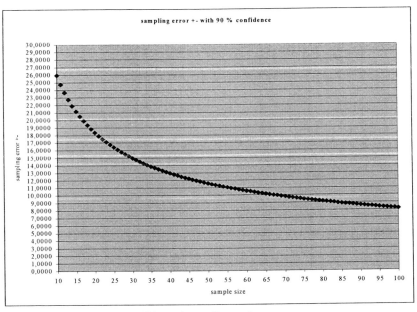

Graph 2b. margin of error at 90 % confidence in small samples.

The ESS data are based on true random samples of the European populations that could adequately work with the complex, European-wide questionnaire (sufficient language capabilities). The religion or denomination variable included - 1 Catholic, 2 Protestant, 3 Eastern Orthodox, 4 other Christian, 5 Jewish, 6 Islam, 7 Eastern religions, and 8 for the other non-Christian religions. Working with small sub samples from larger random samples entails a certain methodological risk, very well known in survey research. The margin of error at 90 % confidence is approximately determined by the formula[3]:

(4) margin of error at 90 % confidence = 0.82 / (n^0.5)

We thus arrive at the following margins of errors for our sub samples (Graph 2a to Graph 2c).

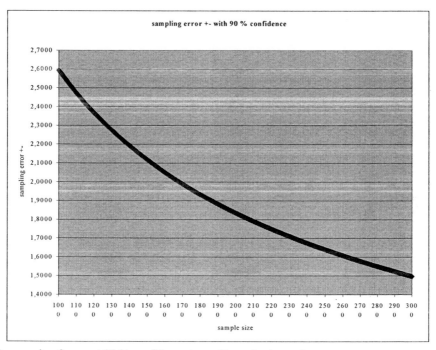

Graph 2c. margin of error at 90 % confidence in medium-sized samples.

The sample sizes and main results for the left-right political scale are reproduced in the appendix, error margins can be immediately concluded from the size of n in the appendix and Graphs 2a – 2c. We excluded cases, where the number of Muslim interview partners for the ESS teams were 5 representative persons or less.

---

[3] *http://www.reference.com/browse/wiki/Margin_of_error* . Please note that n = sample size

Chapter 4

THE ISLAMIST THREAT IN EUROPE – FIRST GUESS ESTIMATES ON MYTHS AND REALITY

Our report about the ESS results should start with a comparison of the PEW research data on the totalitarian potential among Muslim communities in Europe with our own, new ESS data. With the great European Muslim scholar Bassam Tibi, we differentiate strictly between Islam on the one hand and totalitarian, jihadist Islamism on the other hand. Djihadist Islamism does not only want to establish a state, in which the divine law is above the human law, but it is also ready to fight for this goal with arms (see Jihadism's root in political Islam' by Bassam Tibi; *Internationally Herald Tribune,* August 30, 2005). This being stated, we quickly present Tables 2a and 2b that are the basis of our assessment of the size of the real terrorist threat in Europe, away from myths and fancies.

Of course, it might seem to be heroic to conclude from the PEW studies, which only include Muslims in France, the UK, Germany, and Spain, a solid knowledge on opinions of all the Muslims in all EU-25 countries. But the PEW sample makes valid assumptions about approximately ¾ of all Muslims in Europe, and the ESS samples present an even more complete subsection of presumed realities (9/10).

We now proceed to simply extrapolate our national results from the ESS and from the PEW studies on totalitarian Muslim potential in Europe. The reasons for our relative political optimism in interpreting our results are manifold. Our materials generally confirm that it is also sociologically very valid to distinguish between "Islam" and "Islamism". Our materials render strong support to the hypothesis that *passive support for Islamist radicalism in Europe and the complete distrust in democracy does not exceed 400.000 persons.* While there is an understandable siding by European Muslims with the Arab side in the Middle East conflict, and widespread and lamentable reservations against "Jews" and the state of Israel, low trust in democracy is already far less widespread, and ideological open support for suicide bombings in order "to defend Islam" is only shared by 1/6 of Muslims in Europe. The hard core of open Osama Ben Laden supporters and people who have zero trust in democracy are 2 to 3 percent of all Muslims in Europe, a figure, which by the way neatly corresponds to the figures established by Western intelligence agencies, quoted by the high-ranking United States diplomat Timothy M. Savage in his 2004 article in the *"Washington Quarterly"*. Regrettable as Islamist extremism in Europe might be, it is a far way from alarmist views that present "Islam" in Europe as such as being incompatible with the future of democracy. The overall figures are:

Table 2a. The Islamist threat in Europe - the country weights for the PEW and ESS materials to draw conclusions at the EU-25 level

	total population, 2002	percentage of Muslims	total number of Muslims in 2002 (conservative estimate)	country code	PEW	ESS	country weights Muslim population Europe PEW sample	country weights Muslim population Europe ESS sample
Austria	8048000	4,7	378256	A	NO	YES		0,030119012
Belgium	10333000	3,5	361655	B	NO	YES		0,028797141
Denmark	5374000	3	161220	DK	NO	YES		0,012837304
France	59485000	7,5	4461375	F	YES	YES	0,440160212	0,355241445
Germany	82495000	3,7	3052315	G	YES	YES	0,301142051	0,243043634
Greece	10631000	1,3	138203	GR	NO	YES		0,011004552
Luxembourg	444000	2	8880	LUX	NO	YES		0,000707079
Netherlands	16144000	6	968640	NL	NO	YES		0,077128929
Slovenia	1964000	2,5	49100	SI	NO	YES		0,003909637
Spain	40917000	2,5	1022925	SP	YES	YES	0,100921999	0,081451426
Sweden	8924000	4	356960	SW	NO	YES		0,028423297
UK	59229000	2,7	1599183	UK	YES	YES	0,157775737	0,127336545
Cyprus	765000	0,5	3825					
Czech Republic	10210000	0,2	20420					
Estonia	1358000	0,75	10185					
Finland	5199000	0,2	10398					
Hungary	10159000	0,6	60954					
Ireland	3920000	0,49	19208					
Italy	57690000	1,7	980730					
Latvia	2338000	0,02	468					
Lithuania	3469000	0,6	20814					
Malta	397000	7,6	30172					
Poland	38626000	0,08	30901					
Portugal	10177000	0,35	35620					
Slovakia	5379000	0,05	2690					
Total EU-25	453675000		13785095		10135 798	1255 8712		

Source: our own calculations, based on nationmaster.com, which again is based on United States Department of State, religious freedom data 2003.

Table 2b. The Islamist threat in Europe - the presumed
EU-25 wide results, based on a simple extrapolation of the PEW and ESS materials to draw conclusions at the EU-25 level

	implied population weighted total percentage, EU-25	implied total number, EU-25	source	country coverage of all Muslims residing in the EU-25
% of European Muslims say relations between Muslims and the people in Western countries are bad	56	7678000	PEW	73,53%
% of European Muslims not expressing explicit favorable ratings of Jews	49	6814000	PEW	73,53%
% of European Muslims believe Hamas victory is good for Palestinians	44	6009000	PEW	73,53%
% of European Muslims want to be distinct from society	33	4570000	PEW	73,53%
% of European Muslims expressing low trust in parliament	31	4282000	ESS	91,10%
% of European Muslims expressing low trust in the legal system	26	3518000	ESS	91,10%
% of European Muslims with pronounced left views	24	3371000	ESS	91,10%
% of European Muslims favor Iranian nuclear weapons	23	3211000	PEW	73,53%
% of European Muslims not expressing explicit favorable ratings of Christians	20	2714000	PEW	73,53%
% of European Muslims expressing low trust in the police	19	2624000	ESS	91,10%
% of European Muslims expressing low trust in democracy	15	2003000	ESS	91,10%
% of European Muslims favor suicide bombings (violence is sometimes justified in order to defend Islam)	13	1810000	PEW	73,53%
% of European Muslims who identify with fundamentalists	8	1037000	PEW	73,53%
% of European Muslims with extreme right-wing views	5	622000	ESS	91,10%
% of European Muslims expressing a lot of confidence in Osama Ben Laden	3	394000	PEW	73,53%
% of European Muslims expressing zero trust in democracy	2	316000	ESS	91,10%

Source: our own calculations from PEW and ESS data

Chapter 5

MUSLIM SECULARISM IN EUROPE
OR ECUMENICAL EUROPEAN THEOLOGY
OF GLOBAL PEACE AND JUSTICE?

A traditional answer by western sociology and philosophy to the problem of religion consists in expecting that with progressive "modernization" religious values will diminish in importance. But Inglehart and Norris (2004) show that although members of virtually all advanced industrial societies have been moving toward more secular orientations during the past 50 years, people with traditional religious views constitute a growing proportion of the world's population. Secularization is occurring in Australia, New Zealand, Japan, Canada and Western Europe. Even in the U.S., there has been some movement in this direction. Within most advanced industrial societies, attendance at religious services has fallen during the past several decades. Religious authorities largely have lost their authority to dictate to the public on birth control, divorce, abortion, sexual orientation and the necessity of marriage before childbirth. But this process of secularization is linked with a sharp decline in human fertility rates: As a result, the proportion of the world's population with traditional religious values is growing, not shrinking. Organized religion is losing its grip on the public, but spiritual concerns are taking on growing importance. The Inglehart and Norris findings also show that Moslems are much more likely than Protestants to subscribe to the values associated with the "Protestant work ethic" (Inglehart and Norris, 2004).

Secularism and "protestant" work ethics will characterize in an increasing fashion the cultural landscape of Muslims in Europe. As stated, the reasons for our optimism are manifold. Apart from the fact that open support for radical djihadist Islamism and zero trust in democracy only amounts presumably to 2-3 % of the total European Muslim population, secularism seems to affect not only the European majority culture landscapes, but also a considerable proportion of the European Muslim communities. The well-known statements of political science and sociological modernization theories and world value research again are being confirmed here:

Table 3a. secularism among the majority cultures

	% of total pop 2004 (2002) never attending religious services
EE Estonia	79,3
SE Sweden	73,7
CZ Czech Republic	73,3
BE Belgium	67,4
IS Iceland	62,3
NL Netherlands	62,1
FR France	61,9
NO Norway	59,8
GB United Kingdom	59,2
DE Germany	54,1
DK Denmark	49,6
HU Hungary	47,5
ES Spain	45,3
LU Luxembourg	40,3
CH Switzerland	37,9
AT Austria	36,6
FI Finland	35,8
SI Slovenia	35,6
UA Ukraine	30,3
IT Italy	29,7
SK Slovakia	29,6
IL Israel	26,5
PT Portugal	25,6
IE Ireland	14,6
GR Greece	11,3
PL Poland	9,3

Source: calculated by Christian Bischof, Tomaz Kastrun, Karl Mueller and the author from the data of the ESS, available at *http://www.europeansocialsurvey.org/*

Table 3b. secularism among the Muslim communities

	% of total Muslim pop 2004 (2002) never attending religious Muslim religious services
LU Luxembourg	57,1
SE Sweden	50
SI Slovenia	37,5
GR Greece	33
NL Netherlands	33
ES Spain	30
CH Switzerland	29,2

Table 3b. (Continued)

	% of total Muslim pop 2004 (2002) never attending religious Muslim religious services
AT Austria	23,8
NO Norway	23,8
DK Denmark	21,4
GB United Kingdom	17,5
FR France	17,4
BE Belgium	16,3
DE Germany	11,9
IL Israel	7,4

Source: calculated by Christian Bischof, Tomaz Kastrun, Karl Mueller and the author from the data of the ESS, available at *http://www.europeansocialsurvey.org/*

By far, the secularists are the biggest denominational reality in Europe, and Christianity – with a few exceptions – is already at the margins. This can be shown by analyzing the three biggest denominational/religious subgroups for each European country with the ESS data:

Table 3c. Component analysis of the different denominational and political groups, and their share in total population

	religious practice	frequency rank among denominational groups in the country	% of total population, 2004	DYN denominations, 2002-2004
AT Austria	Roman Catholic: less frequent than every week	1	41,55	4,53
AT Austria	without denomination	2	29,33	-1,95
AT Austria	Roman Catholic: weekly or more frequent	3	12,79	-2,44
BE Belgium	without denomination	1	55,35	3,42
BE Belgium	Roman Catholic: less frequent than every week	2	20,65	-3,6
BE Belgium	Roman Catholic: never	3	11,5	2,81
CH Switzerland	without denomination	1	30,5	-7,35
CH Switzerland	Protestant: less frequent than every week	2	24,75	4,76
CH Switzerland	Roman Catholic: less frequent than every week	3	22,35	1,09
CZ Czech Republic	without denomination	1	69,17	2,86
CZ Czech Republic	Roman Catholic: less frequent than every week	2	15,23	-1,12
CZ Czech Republic	Roman Catholic: weekly or more frequent	3	6,42	-0,77
DE Germany	without denomination	1	46,1	0,4
DE Germany	Protestant: less frequent than every week	2	19,81	-3,84

Table 3c. (Continued)

	religious practice	frequency rank among denominational groups in the country	% of total population, 2004	DYN denomination s, 2002-2004
DE Germany	Roman Catholic: less frequent than every week	3	14,83	1,45
DK Denmark	Protestant: less frequent than every week	1	44,03	5,79
DK Denmark	without denomination	2	36,62	-5,2
DK Denmark	Protestant: never	3	12,52	-2,21
EE Estonia	without denomination	1	78,15	xx
EE Estonia	Orthodox: less frequent than every week	2	8,9	xx
EE Estonia	Protestant: less frequent than every week	3	6,51	xx
ES Spain	Roman Catholic: less frequent than every week	1	34,73	-3,71
ES Spain	without denomination	2	26,72	3,74
ES Spain	Roman Catholic: never	3	18,21	0,6
FI Finland	Protestant: less frequent than every week	1	57,8	xx
FI Finland	without denomination	2	24,11	xx
FI Finland	Protestant: never	3	11,48	xx
FR France	without denomination	1	49,64	-0,91
FR France	Roman Catholic: less frequent than every week	2	25,32	xx
FR France	Roman Catholic: never	3	11,24	xx
GB United Kingdom	without denomination	1	48,8	-1,01
GB United Kingdom	Protestant: less frequent than every week	2	12,74	-5,6
GB United Kingdom	Protestant: never	3	7,95	-2,43
GR Greece	Orthodox: less frequent than every week	1	63,48	-3,08
GR Greece	Orthodox: weekly or more frequent	2	23,42	-1,19
GR Greece	without denomination	3	9,09	5,86
HU Hungary	without denomination	1	36,7	0,57
HU Hungary	Roman Catholic: less frequent than every week	2	28,54	xx
HU Hungary	Protestant: less frequent than every week	3	11,44	xx
IE Ireland	Roman Catholic: weekly or more frequent	1	55,45	6,48
IE Ireland	Roman Catholic: less frequent than every week	2	25,79	-0,58
IE Ireland	without denomination	3	12,4	-4,29
IS Iceland	without denomination	1	51,78	xx
IS Iceland	Protestant: less frequent than every week	2	30,77	xx
IS Iceland	Protestant: never	3	10,51	xx

Table 3c. (Continued)

	religious practice	frequency rank among denominational groups in the country	% of total population, 2004	DYN denominations, 2002-2004
IT Italy	Roman Catholic: less frequent than every week	1	41,18	xx
IT Italy	Roman Catholic: weekly or more frequent	2	27,59	xx
IT Italy	without denomination	3	23,74	xx
LU Luxembourg	Roman Catholic: less frequent than every week	1	33,11	6,15
LU Luxembourg	without denomination	2	30,3	3,67
LU Luxembourg	Roman Catholic: weekly or more frequent	3	9,7	-1,4
NL Netherlands	without denomination	1	53,88	-2,77
NL Netherlands	Roman Catholic: less frequent than every week	2	14,85	1,01
NL Netherlands	Protestant: weekly or more frequent	3	7,37	0,54
NO Norway	without denomination	1	48,19	-0,82
NO Norway	Protestant: less frequent than every week	2	30,36	-2,75
NO Norway	Protestant: never	3	9,42	-0,19
PL Poland	Roman Catholic: weekly or more frequent	1	56,21	2,37
PL Poland	Roman Catholic: less frequent than every week	2	33,12	-1,83
PL Poland	without denomination	3	8,06	-0,13
PT Portugal	Roman Catholic: less frequent than every week	1	44,96	2,36
PT Portugal	Roman Catholic: weekly or more frequent	2	26,13	-0,03
PT Portugal	without denomination	3	15,33	-1,7
SE Sweden	without denomination	1	68,21	-1,96
SE Sweden	Protestant: less frequent than every week	2	20,29	-7,12
SE Sweden	Protestant: never	3	5,07	-1,9
SI Slovenia	Roman Catholic: less frequent than every week	1	27,95	1,59
SI Slovenia	without denomination	2	22,24	-28,38
SI Slovenia	Roman Catholic: never	3	12,57	9,73
SK Slovakia	Roman Catholic: less frequent than every week	1	27,69	xx
SK Slovakia	Roman Catholic: weekly or more frequent	2	27,04	xx
SK Slovakia	without denomination	3	24,78	xx
UA Ukraine	Orthodox: less frequent than every week	1	46,65	xx
UA Ukraine	without denomination	2	25,77	xx
UA Ukraine	Orthodox: weekly or more frequent	3	6,33	xx

Source: calculated by Christian Bischof, Tomaz Kastrun, Karl Mueller and the author from the data of the ESS, available at *http://www.europeansocialsurvey.org/*

Only in Ireland and in Poland, regular Sunday Catholic religious service attendance constitutes the dominant social practice of a European country, and Protestant regular Sunday Church attendance rates fare even worse and only in the Netherlands and in the UK, they are only above 5 % of total population. By any standards, secularism defined as belonging to no religious group is now the dominant "denomination" in a majority of European countries, and number 2 or number 3 in an equally astonishing manner:

Table 3d. "Pagan" Europe?

	religious practice	frequency rank among denominational groups in the country	% of total population, 2004	DYN denomination s, 2002-2004
EE Estonia	without denomination	1	78,15	xx
CZ Czech Republic	without denomination	1	69,17	2,86
SE Sweden	without denomination	1	68,21	-1,96
BE Belgium	without denomination	1	55,35	3,42
NL Netherlands	without denomination	1	53,88	-2,77
IS Iceland	without denomination	1	51,78	xx
FR France	without denomination	1	49,64	-0,91
GB United Kingdom	without denomination	1	48,8	-1,01
NO Norway	without denomination	1	48,19	-0,82
DE Germany	without denomination	1	46,1	0,4
HU Hungary	without denomination	1	36,7	0,57
CH Switzerland	without denomination	1	30,5	-7,35
DK Denmark	without denomination	2	36,62	-5,2
LU Luxembourg	without denomination	2	30,3	3,67
AT Austria	without denomination	2	29,33	-1,95
ES Spain	without denomination	2	26,72	3,74
UA Ukraine	without denomination	2	25,77	xx
FI Finland	without denomination	2	24,11	xx
SI Slovenia	without denomination	2	22,24	-28,38
SK Slovakia	without denomination	3	24,78	xx
IT Italy	without denomination	3	23,74	xx
PT Portugal	without denomination	3	15,33	-1,7
IE Ireland	without denomination	3	12,4	-4,29
GR Greece	without denomination	3	9,09	5,86
PL Poland	without denomination	3	8,06	-0,13

Source: calculated by Christian Bischof, Tomaz Kastrun, Karl Mueller and the author from the data of the ESS, available at *http://www.europeansocialsurvey.org/* .

Muslim weekly prayer attendance rates were, on average for the period 2002-2004, just about 1/3 of total Muslim (European) population or even below in the following countries (ranked by their rates of Muslim "secularism"): Luxembourg, Sweden, France, Slovenia, Belgium, Austria, Norway, Spain, Denmark, the Netherlands, Germany, Israel, and in Greece. Only Swiss and British Muslims were, on average, more observant of their weekly regular prayers in their Mosques, but even here one could remark that several Christian groups, so in the Ukraine, Portugal, Spain, Ireland, Poland, Italy, the Czech Republic, Slovkia, the UK, Netherlands, and Switzerland were more observant than British or Swiss Muslims.

Table 3e. religious practice (weekly or more frequent religious service attendance rate per total membership of the denominational group)

	N = 2002	N = 2004	% regular obvervants in % of the religious group 2002	% regular obvervants in % of the religious group 2004	DYN religious observance, 2002-2004	country code	average observation rate, 2002 – 2004
Orthodox	20	9	20,00	0,00	-20,00	AT	10,00
Protestant	66	63	9,09	14,29	5,19	AT	11,69
Muslim	16	21	25,00	14,29	-10,71	AT	19,64
Roman Catholic	1149	1188	25,85	20,96	-4,89	AT	23,40
Muslim	28	49	14,29	22,45	8,16	BE	18,37
Roman Catholic	692	632	22,25	18,20	-4,06	BE	20,23
Protestant	8	10	12,50	40,00	27,50	BE	26,25
Orthodox	xx	xx	xx	xx	xx	BE	xx
Orthodox	7	18	0,00	5,56	5,56	CH	2,78
Protestant	484	649	6,40	12,33	5,92	CH	9,37
Roman Catholic	568	625	19,37	21,12	1,75	CH	20,24
Muslim	9	24	55,56	20,83	-34,72	CH	38,19
Protestant	44	68	20,45	16,18	-4,28	CZ	18,32
Roman Catholic	343	620	25,66	25,65	-0,01	CZ	25,65
Orthodox	xx	6	xx	50,00	xx	CZ	50,00
Muslim	xx	xx	xx	xx	xx	CZ	xx
Protestant	801	685	5,87	7,59	1,72	DE	6,73
Orthodox	14	18	14,29	5,56	-8,73	DE	9,92
Roman Catholic	533	581	22,89	20,14	-2,75	DE	21,51
Muslim	41	42	17,07	38,10	21,02	DE	27,58
Protestant	765	817	3,14	3,79	0,66	DK	3,47
Roman Catholic	9	17	11,11	5,88	-5,23	DK	8,50
Muslim	17	14	11,76	28,57	16,81	DK	20,17
Orthodox	xx	xx	xx	xx	xx	DK	xx
Orthodox	xx	158	xx	9,49	xx	EE	9,49
Roman Catholic	xx	10	xx	10,00	xx	EE	10,00
Protestant	xx	135	xx	20,74	xx	EE	20,74
Muslim	xx	xx	xx	xx	xx	EE	xx
Orthodox	xx	6	xx	16,67	xx	ES	16,67

Table 3e. (Continued)

	N = 2002	N = 2004	% regular obvervants in % of the religious group 2002	% regular obvervants in % of the religious group 2004	DYN religious observance, 2002-2004	country code	average observation rate, 2002 – 2004
Muslim	xx	10	xx	20,00	xx	ES	20,00
Roman Catholic	1051	976	25,50	23,46	-2,04	ES	24,48
Protestant	xx	7	60,00	71,43	11,43	ES	65,71
Orthodox	20	xx	5,00	xx	xx	FI	5,00
Protestant	1379	xx	5,00	xx	xx	FI	5,00
Muslim	xx	xx	xx	xx	xx	FI	xx
Roman Catholic	xx	xx	xx	xx	xx	FI	xx
Muslim	46	xx	8,70	xx	xx	FR	8,70
Protestant	21	xx	14,29	xx	xx	FR	14,29
Roman Catholic	607	xx	15,32	xx	xx	FR	15,32
Orthodox	xx	xx	xx	xx	xx	FR	xx
Orthodox	xx	6	xx	16,67	xx	GB	16,67
Protestant	648	446	17,59	20,63	3,04	GB	19,11
Muslim	27	40	33,33	40,00	6,67	GB	36,67
Roman Catholic	175	181	44,57	40,33	-4,24	GB	42,45
Roman Catholic	7	15	28,57	20,00	-8,57	GR	24,29
Orthodox	1858	1728	26,26	26,39	0,12	GR	26,33
Protestant	7	xx	28,57	xx	xx	GR	28,57
Muslim	34	21	23,53	42,86	19,33	GR	33,19
Protestant	234	xx	9,83	xx	xx	HU	9,83
Roman Catholic	625	xx	20,32	xx	xx	HU	20,32
Muslim	xx	xx	xx	xx	xx	HU	xx
Orthodox	xx	xx	xx	xx	xx	HU	xx
Protestant	54	58	51,85	44,83	-7,02	IE	48,34
Roman Catholic	1324	1601	62,69	66,46	3,77	IE	64,57
Muslim	xx	xx	xx	xx	xx	IE	xx
Orthodox	xx	xx	xx	xx	xx	IE	xx
Roman Catholic	86	xx	17,44	xx	xx	IL	17,44
Muslim	323	xx	30,34	xx	xx	IL	30,34
Orthodox	xx	xx	xx	xx	xx	IL	xx
Protestant	xx	xx	xx	xx	xx	IL	xx
Protestant	xx	232	xx	5,17	xx	IS	5,17
Muslim	xx	xx	xx	xx	xx	IS	xx
Orthodox	xx	xx	xx	xx	xx	IS	xx

Roman Catholic	xx	xx	xx	xx	xx	IS	xx
Roman Catholic	697	xx	37,02	xx	xx	IT	37,02
Protestant	8	xx	50,00	xx	xx	IT	50,00
Muslim	xx	xx	xx	xx	xx	IT	xx
Orthodox	xx	xx	xx	xx	xx	IT	xx
Protestant	12	10	0,00	0,00	0,00	LU	0,00
Muslim	16	7	6,25	0,00	-6,25	LU	3,13
Roman Catholic	619	705	21,49	18,58	-2,90	LU	20,03
Orthodox	6	xx	33,33	xx	xx	LU	33,33
Roman Catholic	449	408	16,26	16,18	-0,08	NL	16,22
Muslim	36	21	25,00	19,05	-5,95	NL	22,02
Protestant	367	318	41,96	41,19	-0,77	NL	41,58
Orthodox	xx	xx	xx	xx	xx	NL	xx
Protestant	904	755	6,08	6,62	0,54	NO	6,35
Orthodox	xx	7	xx	14,29	xx	NO	14,29
Roman Catholic	13	17	7,69	23,53	15,84	NO	15,61
Muslim	18	21	11,11	28,57	17,46	NO	19,84
Orthodox	12	8	25,00	0,00	-25,00	PL	12,50
Roman Catholic	1580	1246	59,87	62,12	2,25	PL	61,00
Muslim	xx	xx	xx	xx	xx	PL	xx
Protestant	xx	xx	xx	xx	xx	PL	xx
Roman Catholic	957	1115	32,92	32,11	-0,81	PT	32,51
Protestant	11	6	81,82	83,33	1,52	PT	82,58
Muslim	xx	xx	xx	xx	xx	PT	xx
Orthodox	xx	xx	xx	xx	xx	PT	xx
Muslim	25	12	8,00	0,00	-8,00	SE	4,00
Roman Catholic	18	19	0,00	15,79	15,79	SE	7,89
Protestant	473	511	12,47	8,02	-4,45	SE	10,25
Orthodox	9	7	0,00	28,57	28,57	SE	14,29
Muslim	12	8	8,33	12,50	4,17	SI	10,42
Orthodox	14	13	7,14	15,38	8,24	SI	11,26
Protestant	xx	9	xx	22,22	xx	SI	22,22
Roman Catholic	538	509	35,13	17,68	-17,45	SI	26,41
Protestant	xx	87	xx	22,99	xx	SK	22,99
Orthodox	xx	14	xx	35,71	xx	SK	35,71
Roman Catholic	xx	722	xx	46,26	xx	SK	46,26
Muslim	xx	xx	xx	xx	xx	SK	xx
Orthodox	xx	757	xx	11,10	xx	UA	11,10

Table 3e. (Continued)

	N = 2002	N = 2004	% regular obvervants in % of the religious group 2002	% regular obvervants in % of the religious group 2004	DYN religious observance, 2002-2004	country code	average observation rate, 2002 – 2004
Roman Catholic	xx	143	xx	38,46	xx	UA	38,46
Protestant	xx	19	xx	89,47	xx	UA	89,47
Muslim	xx	xx	xx	xx	xx	UA	xx

Note: only subgroups with n > 5.0 were evaluated. Source: calculated by Christian Bischof, Tomaz Kastrun, Karl Mueller and the author from the data of the ESS, available at *http://www.europeansocialsurvey.org/*

For all countries and sub-regions of the world system, there is a fairly regular tendency for more developed states to show a higher degree of "secularization" (lower regular religious service attendance rates). As we will further develop in Chapter 7, "secularism" does not have to be the only answer, though.

Confronted with the deep human desire for spirituality and eternal values, the process of never-ending secularization finds an impasse. Rejecting the culturalist and exclusivist project of a *"Christian fortress Europe"* that is at the basis of the recent utterly unacceptable remarks by Pope Benedict XVI on Islam and the Prophet Mohammed[1], it is time to spell out anew the

---

[1] The catastrophic sentence, together with the rest of this speech, is to be found at: *http://www.vatican.va/holy_father/benedict_xvi/speeches/2006/september/documents/hf_ben-xvi_spe_ 20060912_university-regensburg_ge.html* The Pope's reference to the by now rightly famous and unacceptable quotation is an incredible step backwards from the days of the Second Vatican Council, that specifically praised Islam in the following fashion:

"The Church regards with esteem also the Moslems. They adore the one God, living and subsisting in Himself; merciful and all- powerful, the Creator of heaven and earth, who has spoken to men; they take pains to submit wholeheartedly to even His inscrutable decrees, just as Abraham, with whom the faith of Islam takes pleasure in linking itself, submitted to God. Though they do not acknowledge Jesus as God, they revere Him as a prophet. They also honor Mary, His virgin Mother; at times they even call on her with devotion. In addition, they await the day of judgment when God will render their deserts to all those who have been raised up from the dead. Finally, they value the moral life and worship God especially through prayer, almsgiving and fasting. Since in the course of centuries not a few quarrels and hostilities have arisen between Christians and Moslems, this sacred synod urges all to forget the past and to work sincerely for mutual understanding and to preserve as well as to promote together for the benefit of all mankind social justice and moral welfare, as well as peace and freedom."(see http://www.dialog.org/dialog/nostra-eng.html).

The present author allows himself to remind the Muslim readership of this article of a few things in this context:

1. the old conflicts of Cardenal Ratzinger with liberation theology and the theologies of the South, which imply the lamentable apparent and present inability of the Pope to engage into a true dialogue with the world's South. Among the sharpest criticism voiced against the new Pope came from liberation theologian Leonardo Boff from Brazil (see*: http://www.causapopular.com.ar/article375.html*)

2. his long-standing, lamentable opposition to Turkish entry into the European Union, which must have been known to the other Cardenals who elected him (see also: *http://www.lefigaro.fr/international/ 20060915.FIG000000254_les_musulmans_choques_par_les_propos_du_pape.html*)

3. the recent apparent sidelining of liberal advisers on Islam in the Vatican in favour of hardliners, which was documented, among others, *in http://www.chiesa.espressonline.it/dettaglio.jsp?id=45084&eng=y*

4. the not too distant publication, when Pope Benedict XVI was Cardenal in the Vatican, in a "revisionist" hard-core German nationalist Austrian publication, *"Aula",* which with justifaction is criticized again and again as an important vehicle of the Neo-Nazi scenery in Europe (see the Documentation archive of the Austrian Resistance Movement at: *http://www.doew.at/projekte/rechts/ chronik/ 1998_11/*

1848aula.html ; evidence is also available from Aula's own website at: *http://www.dieaula.at /buchdienst.htm* The editor of that book is Dr. Otto Scrinzi, a very well-known figure in the Austrian extremist right wing scenary: (see also *http://lexikon.idgr.de/s/s_c/scrinzi-otto/scrinzi-otto.php*).

A most valuable source of information is Armstrong (2006). Readers of this publication are being asked to be patient with this long quotation, but it the central point of today's situation, end-September 2006. Among the central points, Professor Armstrong makes, are:

"We were posing as a tolerant society, yet passing judgment from a position of extremes and irrationality". (...) "September 11th has confirmed a view of Islam that is centuries old, which is that Islam is inherently violent and intolerant of others" (...) "The events have been a great shock to the Americans, and they are now in a state of numbness and depression," Armstrong explained. " (...) "On the East Coast where I spent most of my time, people descended en masse on the bookstores and took off the shelves everything they could find about Islam. While some did this to confirm old prejudices and fears -- depending on who you choose to read -- the majority was keen on learning about Islam." (...) The key question would be, "why do they hate us?" Armstrong said, followed by others, such as: "What do Muslims think of Christians and Jews? Is Islam an inherently violent religion? Why do we always hear bad rhetoric about Christians? What about women in Islam? Is Islam against modernity?" (...) In responding to such questions, Armstrong walks a fine line between deconstructing long- held stereotypes while at the same time not becoming apologetic. She noted that there are differences in the way her views are received in the US and in Europe. "One of the good things about the Americans is that they do like to know," she says. "There is earnestness about them that one does not observe in a European society such as Holland, for example. They are open to criticism in a way that does not exist in Europe, where people assume they know it all." (...)

"Anti-Islamic doctrine is in-built in the Western ethos that was formulated during the Crusades," she says. "This was the period when the Western world was re-defining itself. The 11th century marked the end of the Dark Ages in Europe and the beginnings of the new Europe. The Crusades were the first co-operative act on the part of the whole new Europe, and the whole crusading ethos shaped the psyche of the key actors performing at this crucial time." (...) "Islam was the quintessential foreigner, and people resented Islam in Europe much as people in the Third World resent the US today. One could say that Islam then was the greatest world power, and it remained so up until the early years of the Ottoman empire. Muslims were everywhere in the Middle East, Turkey,.Iran, South- East Asia, China. Wherever people went, there was Islam, and it was powerful, and people felt it as a threat." (...) "The period of the Crusades was a crucial historical moment during which the West was defining itself, and Islam became a yardstick against which it measured itself. " Islam was everything that the West thought it was not, and it was at the time of the Crusades that the idea that Islam was essentially a violent religion took hold in the West. "Europe was projecting anxiety about its own behaviour onto Islam, and it did the same thing too with the Jewish people," Armstrong said. Even in non-religious societies such as England, Armstrong believes that prejudice against Islam remains, saying that "I think it is in-built into people that Islam is a violent religion." These hostile feelings were given a new lease of life during the colonial period, Armstrong believes, since many of the colonised countries were Muslim countries, and the colonial powers saw in them what they regarded as 'backwardness', attributing this to Islam.

Although she feels that university campuses are almost the only places in the US where big questions are asked, Armstrong says that the events of 11 September divided US academics into two camps. The first camp, led by Martin Kramer, head of the Near and Middle East Studies Institute in Washington DC, accused Armstrong, together with academics such as John Esposito, head of Islamic-Christian Dialogue at Georgetown University, of 'duping' people into believing that Islam was not a threat, an argument Kramer claimed had been proved wrong by the attacks. Only a few weeks after 11 September, Kramer wrote an article, Ivory Towers Built on Sand, in which he put the blame squarely on academics for failing to predict the atrocities. Armstrong explains how the media in the US attempted to silence opposing voices after 11 September. For example, she had been commissioned by the New Yorker magazine to write an article on Islam, but the article was killed and the magazine published one by the academic Bernard Lewis instead. "They thought I am an apologist for Muslims, because my article was about the prophet as a peacemaker, and this did not suit their agenda as much as Lewis's did. Both Lewis and Kramer are staunch Zionists who write from a position of extreme bias. But people need to know that Islam is a universal religion, and that there is nothing aggressively oriental or anti-Western about it. Lewis's line, on the other hand, is that Islam is an inherently violent religion," she said.

"We have to take the extreme right- wing groups very seriously," she says. "This is the European form of fundamentalism; because we don't express discontent in a religious form it comes out in a right-wing way. It's the desire to belong to a clearly defined group combined with a pernicious fear of the other -- a sense of pent-up rage and disappointment with multi-cultural society giving way to this kind of emotion, which feeds into fundamentalism."

counter-project of *"liberation theology"* in a global and in a pan-European and ecumenical fashion. The alternative would be a *European ecumenical theology of global peace and justice* that challenges the present ongoing hegemonistic project of the United States of America and that links the forces opposing the ongoing wars, especially the one in Iraq, in

---

Armstrong's Muhammad: a Biography of the Prophet has sold millions of copies since it appeared in 1996, and she has become used to accusations of being "an apologist for Islam", while not taking much notice of such rhetoric. "It is very nice that people think that the book was written by a Muslim," she says, "but what a religious scholar tries to do is to enter into a religion by a leap of the imagination, in order to understand not just the beliefs, or the history and doctrine, but also the underlying feel of the religion, and I try to do this with all religions and not just with Islam. I did the same when I wrote the history of Judaism, and I am doing the same now that I am writing a biography of the Buddha."

Armstrong is currently also working on a history of the period from 800 BC to 200 AD when many great world faiths came into being. "Europe," she says, "is about the only place where religion does not matter much. People in Europe might need to rinse their minds of all their bad and lazy theology. People in Europe have not yet asked the big questions about religion; they have tried get rid of primitive forms of religion, but very often what we see in the churches today is exactly the kind of religion that these people are trying to get rid of... Jesus would be horrified by the practices of the church today. I would love to show him around the Vatican, when Christians cannot even share a church together. He would be appalled, much as Mohamed would be appalled if he knew that September 11th was done in the name of Islam." (...)

How does she think that the Western world and Islam can come together? Is there any common ground between them? Armstrong believes that both sides should try and deal with the extremism in their midst. (...) "Similarly, the West has got to learn that it shares the planet with equals and not with inferiors. This means giving equal space in a conflict such as that between Israel and Palestine. It doesn't mean just using governments to get oil: you promote Saddam Hussein one day, and the next day he becomes public enemy number one. The West promoted people like the Shah of Iran simply because of its greed for oil, even though he had committed atrocities against his own people. There should be no more double standards, because double standards are colonialism in a new form. Western people have also got to disassociate themselves from inherited prejudices about Islam." (...) "Muslims can run a modern state in an Islamic way, and this is what the West has got to see... There are all kinds of ways in which people can be modern, and Muslims should be allowed to come to modernity on their own terms and make a distinctive Islamic contribution to it." (Source: http://www.islamfortoday.com/karenarmstrong02.htm)

favor of a global order that is based on international law, the United Nations, and respect for the different cultures of spirituality around the globe (see the different essays, starting from the cultural traditions of Christianity, Islam, Judaism, and Marxism in Tausch, *et al.* 2000). One cannot underestimate the *possible catalyst role of Euro-Islam in that context:* challenging neo-liberal and hegemonistic globalization in favor of a European Union characterized by cultural tolerance, social justice, and an openness towards *increased cooperation with and migration from the Mediterranean partner countries of the European Union. A positive attitude towards a successful accession process of the Turkish Republic to the European Union is a sine qua non in such a political counter-project*In appendix 1 to 5, and in appendix 13, we further analyze the religious or secular landscape of the European countries and Israel, which, as we stressed, forms part and parcel of the ESS survey effort. Further reference to these data will be made in Chapter 7, which deals with the conclusions to be drawn for policy makers.

Chapter 6

EUROPEAN MUSLIM COMMUNITIES AND THE LISBON PROCESS – COMPARATIVE RESULTS FROM THE EUROPEAN SOCIAL SURVEY

The first, and sad fact that we have to state in this context is that discriminatory policies in the last years seem to have increased poverty among the Muslim communities in Austria, Belgium, Denmark, Germany, Greece, Luxembourg, the Netherlands, Sweden, and Switzerland, while Norway, Slovenia, Spain and the UK reduced Muslim poverty from 2002 to 2004.

Table 4a. Poverty among Muslims in the ESS countries, 2002 and 2004

	very difficult on present income + difficult on present income, 2002	very difficult on present income + difficult on present income, 2004
Austria Muslims	36,7	46,5
Belgium Muslims	26,4	46,5
Denmark Muslims	19	25,1
France Muslims	79,6	
Germany Muslims	28,1	47,7
Greece Muslims	80,2	82,8
Israel Muslims	47,4	
Luxembourg Muslims	38,4	47,8
Netherlands Muslims	30,8	53,6
Norway Muslims	35	27,3
Slovenia Muslims	21,1	10
Spain Muslims	66,6	64
Sweden Muslims	26,1	28,6
Switzerland Muslims	7,7	56,6
UK Muslims	27,8	27,1

Source: estimated by the author, based on the data calculations provided by Christian Bischof, Tomaz Kastrun, Karl Mueller and the author from the data of the ESS, available at *http://www. europeansocialsurvey.org/*

Likewise, poverty among the non-Muslim population seems to have increased in Belgium, Germany, Luxembourg, the Netherlands, Norway, Switzerland and in the UK, while in Austria, Denmark, Greece, Slovenia, Spain and Sweden, poverty seems to have decreased in the time period between 2002 and 2004.

Table 4b. Poverty among non Muslims in the ESS countries, 2002 and 2004

	very difficult on present income + difficult on present income, 2002	very difficult on present income + difficult on present income, 2004
Austria non-Muslims	18,3	12
Belgium non-Muslims	15,4	21,9
Denmark non-Muslims	5,1	3,9
France non-Muslims	44	no data
Germany non-Muslims	10,7	14,8
Greece non-Muslims	51,9	50,4
Israel non-Muslims	39,5	no data
Luxembourg non-Muslims	9,7	11,3
Netherlands non-Muslims	9,6	12,9
Norway non-Muslims	7,7	9,2
Slovenia non-Muslims	17,4	14,1
Spain non-Muslims	21,8	18
Sweden non-Muslims	8,7	8,6
Switzerland non-Muslims	8,2	12,1
UK non-Muslims	12,2	17

Source: estimated by the author, based on the data calculations provided by Christian Bischof, Tomaz Kastrun, Karl Mueller and the author from the data of the ESS, available at *http://www.european socialsurvey.org/*

To calibrate our ESS measures of poverty, we compared the maximally time-matched ESS poverty rates with the UNDP Human development index, with life expectancy at birth (UNDP), with Eurostat poverty rates, and with the UNDP/OECD measure no survival to age 60, and the percentage of the population below the 50 % of median income threshold. While ESS-non-Muslim poverty rates correlate closely with the UNDP Human Development Index, Muslim poverty rates indeed correlate highly with the overall Eurostat poverty rate. 27 % of the variance of Eurostat poverty rates in Europe is already being explained by Muslim poverty rates.

Using the ESS cross-national and quantitative data, we first estimate a new UNDP-type index of *"Muslim development"* in Europe, based on the ESS indicators

- the percentage of the Muslim community living above poverty
- the percentage of the Muslim community expressing some or great trust (levels 4 to 10 on the ESS scale) in democracy

- the percentage of the Muslim community expressing some or great trust (levels 4 to 10 on the ESS scale) in legal system
- the percentage of the Muslim community expressing some or great trust (levels 4 to 10 on the ESS scale) in parliament
- the percentage of the Muslim community expressing some or great trust (levels 4 to 10 on the ESS scale) in the police

Table 4c. Other Poverty Indicators

	UNDP HDI	UNDP Life expectancy	Eurostat poverty rate	OECD poverty rate< 50 % median income	no survival to age 60
Austria	0,936	79	13	8	9,1
Belgium	0,945	78,9	15	8	9,4
Denmark	0,941	77,2	11	9,2	10,4
France	0,938	79,5	12	8	9,8
Germany	0,93	78,7	16	8,3	8,8
Greece	0,912	78,3	20		9,2
Israel	0,915	79,7		13,5	7,7
Luxembourg	0,949	78,5	11	6	9,7
Netherlands	0,943	78,4	12	7,3	8,7
Norway	0,963	79,4	11	6,4	8,4
Slovenia	0,904	76,4	10	8,2	11,8
Spain	0,928	79,5	20	10,1	8,7
Sweden	0,949	80,2	11	6,5	7,2
Switzerland	0,947	80,5		9,3	7,8
UK	0,939	78,4	18	12,5	8,7

Sources: see Table 1c. We took great care to time-match properly, as far as we could, the data with Muslim and overall non-Muslim poverty rates in the ESS survey. French and Israeli data refer to 2002, the rest to 2004.

Table 4d. calibration of the ESS poverty measures

	correlation with non-Muslim poverty	correlation with Muslim poverty
UNDP HDI	*-0,525480595*	-0,121134764
UNDP Life expectancy	0,134261793	0,413331423
Eurostat poverty rate	0,486550285	*0,519410888*
OECD poverty rate< 50 % median income	0,440115634	0,026565342
no survival to age 60	-0,017283814	-0,212872958

Sources: our own comparisons from Tables 1c and 4a – c above.

Likewise, we construct another UNDP type index, which we call *"Muslim empowerment index"*, which measures

- a small difference in the percentage of the non-Muslim communities and the Muslim community of a European country living above poverty
- a small difference in the percentage of the non-Muslim communities and the Muslim community of a European country expressing trust in democracy
- a small difference in the percentage of the non-Muslim communities and the Muslim community of a European country expressing trust in the legal system
- a small difference in the percentage of the non-Muslim communities and the Muslim community of a European country expressing trust in parliament
- a small difference in the percentage of the non-Muslim communities and the Muslim community of a European country expressing trust in the police

From here on, the results of this study can be relatively quickly presented. Our overall indicator of Muslim development in Europe is presented in Table 5a. The best practice countries: printed in *bold letters*. It emerges that the *two multinational states* in Europe *par excellence,* are Switzerland and Belgium, show the best results for the Muslim development indicator, while multinational Belgium and Sweden have the best results for the Muslim empowerment indicator. Austria, France, Germany, the OECD ESS comparison country Israel, and Slovenia are ranked very low on our two main indicators. Thus, in the EU-25 countries Austria, France, Germany, and Slovenia there is a compelling need to improve performance in terms of creating opportunities for increased Muslim participation in the following areas

- democracy
- economy
- legal system
- parliament
- police

Probably the most important single result from this study is the realization that there is a close connection between the Lisbon process and Muslim development in Europe. Using a single Lisbon process indicator that was developed elsewhere in the literature (Tausch, 2006, wiiw) we found that Lisbon process implementation explained more than half of the variance of "Muslim development" in Europe. With other words: the best way, European decision makers can meet the hopes and expectancies of the Muslim communities in Europe, is to implement the Lisbon process properly. Also, there is a very close statistical relationship between the UNDP Human Development Index and the new Muslim Development Index Europe. The relationship explains some 2/5 of the variance of "Muslim development".

Table 5a. The Muslim development index, Europe

	UNDP-type *Muslim development index* Europe (1/5 * each component index)
Switzerland	0,8547
Belgium	0,7003
Denmark	0,6861
Sweden	0,6801
Norway	0,6579
UK	0,6437
Netherlands	0,5874
Greece	0,5714
Luxembourg	0,5621
Germany	0,5410
Austria	0,4943
Israel	0,4038
France	0,3879
Slovenia	0,2182
Spain	0,1441

Source: estimated by the author, based on the data calculations provided by Christian Bischof, Tomaz Kastrun, Karl Mueller and the author from the data of the ESS, available at *http://www.europeansocialsurvey.org/*

Table 5b. the Muslim empowerment index, Europe

	UNDP-type **Muslim empowerment index** Europe (1/5 * each component index)
Belgium	0,8478
Sweden	0,8037
Luxembourg	0,7875
UK	0,7457
Spain	0,6129
Greece	0,5331
Denmark	0,5317
Switzerland	0,5244
Norway	0,4930
Germany	0,4912
Netherlands	0,4819
France	0,4718
Austria	0,4559
Israel	0,4143
Slovenia	0,0567

Source: estimated by the author, based on the data calculations provided by Christian Bischof, Tomaz Kastrun, Karl Mueller and the author from the data of the ESS, available at *http://www.european socialsurvey.org/*

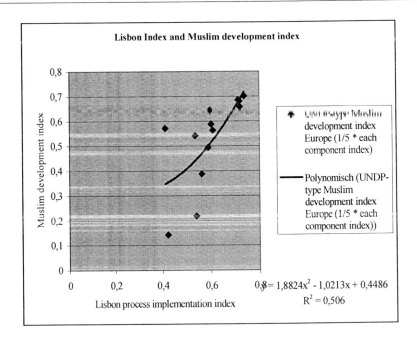

Source: estimated by the author, based on the data calculations provided by Christian Bischof, Tomaz Kastrun, Karl Mueller and the author from the data of the ESS, available at *http://www.europeansocialsurvey.org/*

Graph 3a. The Lisbon process and the Muslim development index

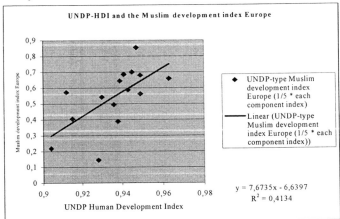

.Source: estimated by the author, based on the data calculations provided by Christian Bischof, Tomaz Kastrun, Karl Mueller and the author from the data of the ESS, available at *http://www.europeansocialsurvey.org/*

Graph 3b. Human development and Muslim development in Europe.

Graph 3c again shows the relevance of the hypotheses and theories put forward by Professor Mancur Olson. Market economies are in a stark contradiction with cast societies; every system that rewards people by a cast principle is at the end of the day doomed to failure. It is no surprise, then, to see that European systems that are characterized by a high and unacceptable degree of gender discrimination are also the ones that strongly discriminate against their Muslim communities, and vice versa.

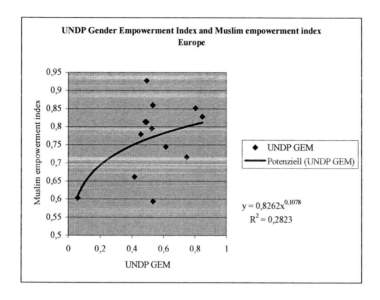

Source: estimated by the author, based on the data calculations provided by Christian Bischof, Tomaz
    Kastrun, Karl Mueller and the author from the data of the ESS, available at
    http://www.europeansocialsurvey.org/
Graph 3c. Overall societal discrimination and the discrimination of Muslims: the interrelationship
between the gender empowerment index and the Muslim empowerment index.

Dynamic aspects in the Muslim integration/discrimination process should not be overlooked. While Spain and Luxembourg at least tried to improve their performance over time, again Austria's performance in the changes of the Muslim development index from 2002 to 2004 was very modest, compared to the already leading position that Belgium and Switzerland had in 2002. Only the Netherlands had a worse performance, then, as Austria, on this indicator; while in Table 6b Austria and the Netherlands also emerge as the relative laggards in implementing Muslim empowerment.

Again, a rather interesting relationship emerges between these newly derived indicators of Muslim performance and the overall political economic processes going on in Europe. Since solid dynamic indicators of the Lisbon process would be very hard to construct in countries outside the EU-25, it might suffice here that we mention the close relationship between the rate of economic growth 1990 – 2003 and the dynamic changes in the Muslim development index from 2002 to 2004. I.e. long-run economic dynamics indeed could change the lot of the Muslim communities of Europe, while Muslims were hardest hit by stagnation and the concomitant unemployment.

Table 6a. the dynamics of the social situation of Muslims in Europe – best or worst increases in the Muslim development index

	UNDP DYN Muslim development index (*0,20 times each component index)
Spain	0,9231
Luxembourg	0,7530
UK	0,5944
Greece	0,5798
Germany	0,5534
Norway	0,5524
Denmark	0,4890
Slovenia	0,4704
Sweden	0,4692
Austria	0,4456
Belgium	0,3475
Netherlands	0,3466
Switzerland	0,2723

Source: estimated by the author, based on the data calculations provided by Christian Bischof, Tomaz Kastrun, Karl Mueller and the author from the data of the ESS, available at *http://www.european socialsurvey.org/*

Table 6b. the dynamics of the social situation of Muslims in Europe – best or worst increases in the Muslim empowerment index

	DYN Muslim empowerment index
Spain	0,8892
Luxembourg	0,8271
UK	0,6851
Germany	0,6458
Norway	0,5979
Greece	0,5961
Sweden	0,5848
Denmark	0,5251
Slovenia	0,5175
Austria	0,4332
Netherlands	0,4032
Belgium	0,3740
Switzerland	0,3030

Source: estimated by the author, based on the data calculations provided by Christian Bischof, Tomaz Kastrun, Karl Mueller and the author from the data of the ESS, available at *http://www.european socialsurvey.org/*

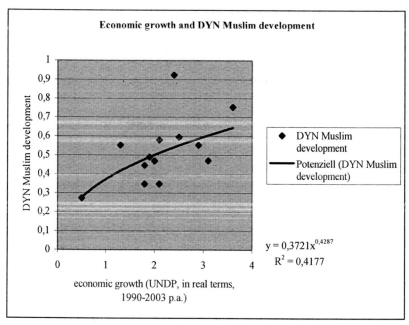

Economic growth and DYN Muslim development

$$y = 0,3721x^{0,4287}$$
$$R^2 = 0,4177$$

Source: estimated by the author, based on the data calculations provided by Christian Bischof, Tomaz
    Kastrun, Karl Mueller and the author from the data of the ESS, available at *http://www.european*
    socialsurvey.org/
Graph 4. Economic growth and increases in the Muslim development index.

Finally, we present in a systematic way the political landscape of the Muslim
communities in Europe and the ESS reference countries. Systematic conclusions about the
relatively straightforward relationship between the political landscape of Muslims in Europe
and the socio-economic Lisbon process are presented in Chapter 7.

By and large, the political attitudes of Muslim communities in Europe, in part to be
explained by the class-context of a large scale Muslim working class migration to Europe
from the beginnings of the 1960s, tend to be left-wing oriented. The large Muslim
communities in Austria, the Netherlands, Switzerland, Belgium, France, Spain (and also in
Israel) tend to share a sizeable segment of far-left political orientations, while the far right
only plays a mayor role in Greece, Denmark and Luxembourg. The Muslim political center is
weakest in Israel, Spain, Luxembourg, Belgium and France, where center, center left and
center right political orientations among the Muslim communities make up 60 % or less of the
total Muslim adult voting age population, studied in the ESS sample. Extreme Muslim left
political orientations even increased in Germany, the Netherlands, Belgium, and the UK,
while the far political right increased its presence among the Muslim communities of
Germany, Sweden, Denmark and Luxembourg. In Denmark, Luxembourg, Greece, Belgium,
Norway and the Netherlands, Muslim political orientations around the center decreased over
time, while in Germany, Sweden, Switzerland, the UK and Austria the weight of the center
increased.

Table 7 and Graphs 5a to 5f present the results in more detail:

Table 7. Political profiles in Europe. General left-right attitudes among the European Muslims and the overall European population, by international comparison

Muslim population	left	moderate left	center	moderate right	right
AT	14,3	23,8	57,1	4,8	0
BE	34,7	18,4	30,6	8,2	8,2
CH	20,8	20,8	45,8	8,3	4,2
DE	14,3	26,2	47,6	9,5	2,4
DK	7,1	35,7	28,6	7,1	21,4
ES	50	10	30	10	0
FR	34,8	26,1	19,6	13	6,5
GB	10	10	65	12,5	2,5
GR	0	9,5	52,4	23,8	14,3
IL	66,3	13,6	13,9	2,8	3,4
LU	0	14,3	42,9	0	42,9
NL	19	33,3	28,6	14,3	4,8
NO	4,8	28,6	33,3	23,8	9,5
SE	8,3	41,7	33,3	8,3	8,3
SI	12,5	12,5	75	0	0
Total Population	left	moderate left	center	moderate right	right
AT	14,5	22,4	41,1	15,4	6,6
BE	11,4	21,7	36,6	22,1	8,1
CH	9	22,7	35,9	22,3	10,1
CZ	13	17	27,1	20	22,9
DE	12,8	28,5	38,9	14,9	4,9
DK	7,1	19,4	27,8	29,7	16
EE	8,6	19,5	39,4	21,2	11,4
ES	18,7	28,3	29,8	14,1	9,1
FI	4,9	16,9	30,7	25,7	21,8
FR	16,8	22,9	30,4	17,4	12,4
GB	7,2	19,5	48,3	17,6	7,4
GR	7,8	14,1	36	19,1	23
HU	12,9	18,8	35,8	18,2	14,2
IE	4,2	17,6	47,1	20,4	10,7
IL	21,5	14,4	20,5	13,8	29,8
IS	9,8	24,2	29,1	24	12,9
IT	15,8	25,3	25,8	20,6	12,4
LU	8,9	17,3	43,5	17	13,4
NL	9,7	23	27,2	28,1	12
NO	8,9	30,3	24	23,5	13,2
PL	9,7	14,5	37,5	19,8	18,5
PT	11,8	28,7	26,2	18,9	14,5
SE	11,6	21,2	27,5	23	16,7
SI	13,3	15,5	42,7	13,6	14,8
SK	15,5	20,9	33,7	15,1	14,7
UA	12,2	11,8	37,5	14,8	23,8

Source: estimated by the author, based on the data calculations provided by Christian Bischof, Tomaz Kastrun, Karl Mueller and the author from the data of the ESS, available at *http://www.european socialsurvey.org/*

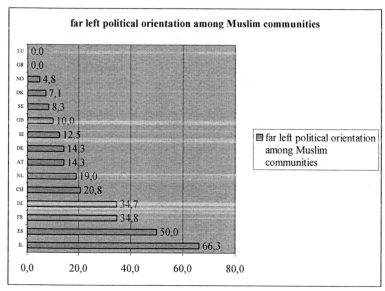

Source: estimated by the author, based on the data calculations provided by Christian Bischof, Tomaz Kastrun, Karl Mueller and the author from the data of the ESS, available at *http://www.european socialsurvey.org/*

Graph 5a. left wing extremism among European Muslims.

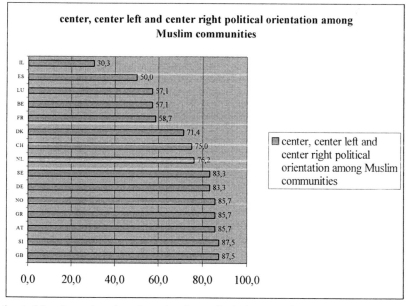

Source: estimated by the author, based on the data calculations provided by Christian Bischof, Tomaz Kastrun, Karl Mueller and the author from the data of the ESS, available at *http://www.european socialsurvey.org/*

Graph 5b. the political center among the Muslim communities in Europe.

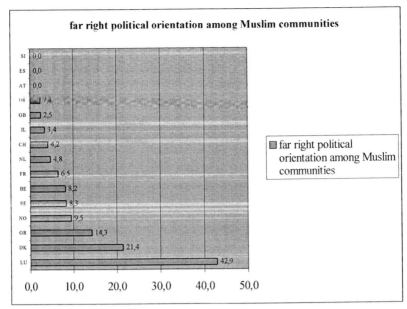

Source: estimated by the author, based on the data calculations provided by Christian Bischof, Tomaz Kastrun, Karl Mueller and the author from the data of the ESS, available at *http://www.european socialsurvey.org/*.

Graph 5c. far right-wing extremism among the Muslim communities in Europe.

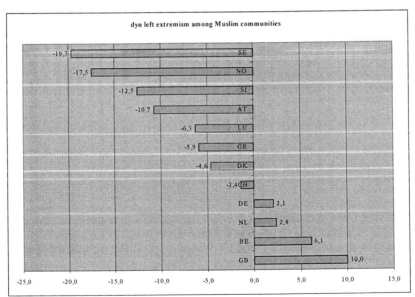

Source: estimated by the author, based on the data calculations provided by Christian Bischof, Tomaz Kastrun, Karl Mueller and the author from the data of the ESS, available at *http://www.europeansocialsurvey.org/*.

Graph 5d: dynamic increases/decreases in % from 2004 to 2004 – left wing extremism among the European Muslim communities.

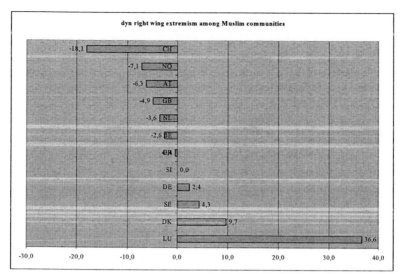

Source: estimated by the author, based on the data calculations provided by Christian Bischof, Tomaz Kastrun, Karl Mueller and the author from the data of the ESS, available at *http://www.europeansocialsurvey.org/*

Graph 5e. dynamic increases/decreases in % from 2004 to 2004 –right wing extremism among the European Muslim communities.

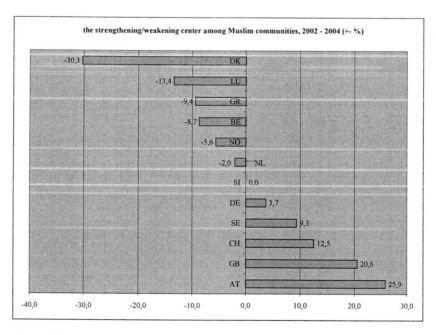

Source: estimated by the author, based on the data calculations provided by Christian Bischof, Tomaz Kastrun, Karl Mueller and the author from the data of the ESS, available at *http://www.europeansocialsurvey.org/* .

Graph 5e. dynamic increases/decreases in % from 2004 to 2004 –center orientation among the European Muslim communities.

Chapter 7

POLITICAL CONCLUSIONS FROM THE ESS RESULTS FOR THE EUROPEAN DECISION MAKERS

This essay made it clear that the key to stability in the *banlieus* is the proper implementation of the Lisbon agenda. There simply **must** be new mechanisms in place that assure the leveling off of the up to now existing very high poverty risks for Europe's "third country" citizens. At the end of the day, mass demand, mass contributions to the social security system, increased profits due to investments in human capital, labor productivity and rising investment levels due to increased mass demand could all be the positive spin-offs of a better integration of the millions of Muslims in Europe. Table 8 once more summarizes the basic tendencies of *"integration policies"* in Europe:

Table 8. Muslim poverty and the poverty risk of foreigners from Third countries in Europe

Ranked by alphabet	Muslims: Income deficit group (columns 3 + 4)	non-Muslims: Income deficit group (columns 3 + 4)	relative poverty risk, Muslims (non-Muslims = 100)	relative poverty risk, non-EU citizens, 1990s (nationwide = 100)
Austria	46,5	12,0	387,5	272,0
Belgium	46,5	21,9	212,3	219,0
Denmark	25,1	3,9	643,6	124,0
France	79,6	44,0	180,9	348,0
Germany	47,7	14,8	322,3	199,0
Greece	82,8	50,4	164,3	124,0
Israel	47,4	39,5	120,0	
Luxembourg	47,8	11,3	423,0	199,0
Netherlands	53,6	12,9	415,5	354,0
Norway	27,3	9,2	296,7	
Slovenia	10,0	14,1	70,9	
Spain	64,0	18,0	355,6	244,0
Sweden	28,6	8,6	332,6	
Switzerland	21,9	12,1	181,0	
UK	27,1	17,0	159,4	116,0

Table 8. (Continued)

Ranked by ocial Apartheid"	Muslims: Income deficit group (columns 3 + 4)	non-Muslims: Income deficit group (columns 3 + 4)	relative poverty risk, Muslims (non-Muslims = 100)	relative poverty risk, non-EU citizens, 1990s (nationwide = 100)
Denmark	75,1	3,9	643,6	124,0
Luxembourg	47,8	11,3	423,0	199,0
Netherlands	53,6	12,9	415,5	354,0
Austria	46,5	12,0	387,5	272,0
Spain	64,0	18,0	355,6	244,0
Sweden	28,6	8,6	332,6	
Germany	47,7	14,8	322,3	199,0
Norway	27,3	9,2	296,7	
Belgium	46,5	21,9	212,3	219,0
Switzerland	21,9	12,1	181,0	
France	79,6	44,0	180,9	348,0
Greece	82,8	50,4	164,3	124,0

Ranked by alphabet	Muslims: Income deficit group (columns 3 + 4)	non-Muslims: Income deficit group (columns 3 + 4)	relative poverty risk, Muslims (non-Muslims = 100)	relative poverty risk, non-EU citizens, 1990s (nationwide = 100)
UK	27,1	17,0	159,4	116,0
Israel	47,4	39,5	120,0	
Slovenia	10,0	14,1	70,9	

Source: calculated by Christian Bischof, Tomaz Kastrun, Karl Mueller and the author from the data of the ESS, available at *http://www.europeansocialsurvey.org/* .

In the following, we try to present some preliminary bi-variety and multivariate analyses to further underline our point. Graph 6 calibrates the use of the UNDP Human Development Index for our further comparisons. This is due to the fact that the OECD country Israel as well as the EFTA/EEA countries Norway and Switzerland, which are part of the ESS sample, of course are not or are not sufficiently covered by the Eurostat data, so that we somehow had to estimate the Israeli, Norwegian and Swiss "Lisbon performance" indirectly. A non-linear formulation, based on the UNDP HDI, would explain some 2/3 of the variance of our Lisbon index, so that the use of the UNDP Human Development Index as a Lisbon process proxy is justified – at least for the moment being.

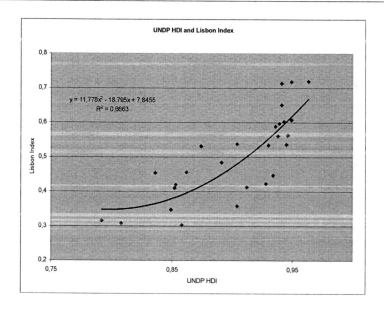

Based on A. Tausch (2006) 'On heroes, villains and statisticians'. The Vienna Institute Monthly Report,
No. 7, July 2006: 20 - 23. Vienna: The Vienna Institute for International Economic Studies (wiiw)
and UNDP HDR 2005.
Graph 6. The UNDP HDI, a combined Lisbon development index, social cohesion and center politics in
Europe.

Graph 7 shows the extent of the Muslim middle and upper class in Europe, as far as it can
be inferred from the statistical materials, contained in the ESS. Sweden, Norway, the UK,
Denmark, Switzerland and Slovenia all have a sizeable Muslim middle or middle and upper
class, while in Greece, France and Spain the middle class is just 1/3 or less of the entire
Muslim population in the country.

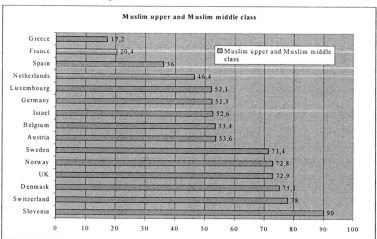

Source: estimated by the author, based on the data calculations provided by Christian Bischof, Tomaz
Kastrun, Karl Mueller and the author from the data of the ESS, available at *http://www.european
socialsurvey.org/*
Graph 7. "Muslim Calvinism", Muslim middle class.

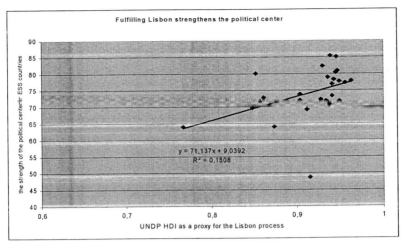

With and without the outlaying case of Israel, whose political dynamics and its Muslim minority within the borders of the year 1948 are a real special case, the relationship between the UNDP HDI as a proxy for the Lisbon process and the formation of a Muslim middle class is quite strong:

Source: estimated by the author, based on the data calculations provided by Christian Bischof, Tomaz Kastrun, Karl Mueller and the author from the data of the ESS, available at *http://www.european socialsurvey.org/* .

Graph 8a. The implementation of the Lisbon process as a requirement for a strong Muslim political middle class – results from the ESS by international comparison.

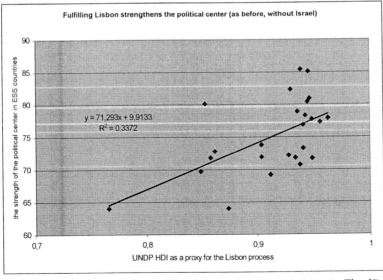

Based on Based on A. Tausch (2006) 'On heroes, villains and statisticians'. *The Vienna Institute Monthly Report,* No. 7, July 2006: 20 - 23. Vienna: The Vienna Institute for International Economic Studies (wiiw) and UNDP HDR 2005, and on our own calculations from ESS, quoted in this work.

Graph 8b. the implementation of the Lisbon process as a requirement for a strong Muslim political middle class – results from the ESS by international comparison without the special case of Israel.

Our hypothesis about a politically stabilizing role that the Muslim middle class could play in Europe, which in turn will be supported by a Lisbon process oriented policy, is further supported by our multivariate analysis reproduced in Table 9. Here, we explain Muslim European political orientation (as documented in Table 7 of this publication) as being determined by the development of a Muslim middle class, by the Muslim development index and the Muslim empowerment index, as well as by the UNDP human development index for the entire country and the prevailing countrywide, general center political orientation. It emerges that the only significant (p<.10) determinant of Muslim political orientation in Europe is the size of the Muslim middle and upper class, affecting significantly the center political orientation of Muslims and reducing left wing extremism (there are no significant predictors for right wing Muslim political extremism):

Table 9. The Multivariate Determinants of Political Center Orientation and Political Extremism Among the Muslim Communities in Europe

	Muslim upper class and middle class	Muslim development index	Muslim empowerment index	UNDP HDI	General pol. orientation center+center left+center right	Constant
Muslim left extremism	-1,26474	181,7859	17,78695	-38,3039	-0,00711	-44,2671
	0,648493	451,6824	32,8271	34,47714	0,258018	393,8853
	0,464556	17,30822				
	1,561695	9				
	2339,219	2696,17				
t-test	-1,95027	0,402464	0,541837	-1,11099	-0,02757	-0,11239
	Muslim upper class and middle class	Muslim development index	Muslim empowerment index	UNDP HDI	general pol. orientation center+center left+center right	constant
Muslim right wing extremism	-0,16993	105,9194	16,6715	6,636208	-0,02999	-88,9321
	0,46744	325,577	23,66208	24,85145	0,185982	283,9163
	0,19336	12,47593				
	0,43148	9				
	335,7968	1400,839				
t-test	-0,36353	0,325328	0,704566	0,267035	-0,16123	-0,31323
	Muslim upper class and middle class	Muslim development index	Muslim empowerment index	UNDP HDI	general pol. orientation center+center left+center right	constant
Muslim center politics	1,436186	-287,885	-34,3575	31,53203	0,036453	233,3008
	0,505964	352,4088	25,61215	26,89954	0,201309	307,3147
	0,60559	13,50411				
	2,763778	9				
	2520,027	1641,249				
t-test	2,838517	-0,81691	-1,34145	1,172215	0,181081	0,759159

Legend: Our entire EXCEL 7.0 calculations are from UNDP and other data sources, quoted above. As in all EXCEL 7.0 outprints, first row: un-standardized regression coefficients, second row: standard errors, second last row: t-Test and direction of the influence. The values immediately below the standard errors are R^2 (third row, left side entry), F, and degrees of freedom (fourth row). Below that: ss reg; ss resid, i.e. the sum of squares of the regression and the sum of squares of the residuals. The right hand entry in the third row is the standard error of the estimate y.

In the light of this analysis, we might ask ourselves who might be the political forces then that might act in solidarity with the large and growing numbers of the Muslim poor in Europe to transform the present tendencies towards marginalization? It is noteworthy that not even the Muslim development index, let alone the Muslim empowerment index, nor the UNDP HDI sufficiently strongly determines Muslim center political orientation in Europe. Why that? The explanation seems to be relatively easy – it is not the extent of poverty as such that causes extremism, but the inability of social systems to provide adequate opportunities for motivated and especially young people to become members of the elite.

That already was a point made by Professor Daniel Pipes, who certainly cannot be accused of siding with Islamist radicals, wrote back in 2002:

> "Moreover, there is a specifically Islamic phenomenon of the faith having been associated with worldly success. Through history, from the Prophet Muhammad's time to the Ottoman Empire a millennium later, Muslims usually had more wealth and more power than other peoples, and were more literate and healthy. With time, Islamic faith came to be associated with worldly well-being-a kind of *Muslim Calvinism*, in effect." (Pipes, 2002)

Various quotations from the literature, above all the striking similarity with the results achieved by the recent ESI report on "Islamic Calvinism" come to one's mind (European Stability Initiative, 2006):

> "[Foreign Minister] Abdullah Gül: "The name of this concept [i.e. of rapid economic growth in the Turkish province of Kayseri] is *Calvinism* in Christianity. In different religions it has different names. They compare the sociological situation in Kayseri to this. They explain it in this way. It is very true." (Turkish Foreign Minister Abdullah Gül, quoted in European Stability Initiative, available at *http://www.esiweb.org/index.php?lang =enandid=114*)

> "BBC: the new entrepreneurialism sweeping across the province is providing an unlikely catalyst for a remarkable religious transformation. A new form of Turkish Islam is emerging here, one which is pro-business and pro-free market, and it's being called Islamic Calvinism. …Critics say it's a Western conspiracy to Christianise Islam, but others have passionately argued in its favour, holding it up as a model for how Islam and modernity can co-exist. One of its most prominent defenders has been Turkey's Deputy Prime Minister, Abdullah Gül, himself a native of Kayseri and the son of an entrepreneur. He sees no contradiction in the term and argues that Turkey can provide a lasting template for a new kind of modern Islam. "The most important thing to ask," he says, is what kind of modernism do we want? Are you living in this world, or are you dreaming? The people of Kayseri are no[t] dreaming - they are realistic, and that's the kind of Islam we need." quoted in European Stability Initiative, available at *http://www.esiweb.org/index.php?lang=enandid=154andnews_ID=72*

Our basically neo-liberal policy conclusion would not contradict the view that in the short- and medium term, a coalition of trade unionists, environmentalists, alter-globalists, minorities, human rights activists and religious "progressives" will be most likely to act in solidarity with Europe's Muslim communities. The old traditions of the ecumenical religious left in Europe before the second World War, which were basically linked to the social democracies, the "Euro-communist" left in the Mediterranean countries of the 1950s, 1960s, and 1970s that always also contained an important religious element, and the liberation theology movement from the "Third World" in the 1980s (Tausch et al., 2000) all have to grapple with the fact that religious practice in the advanced countries of the West dwindles, traditional sectors of the urban, industrial workforce in many European countries have politically shifted to the right, and – above all – traditional "social policies" of the Left most probably will not solve the issues of enterprise creation, middle class development and employment creation for the 15 million or more Muslims in Europe.

In view of the ongoing world political confrontations, especially in Iraq, the support of the anti-war left, especially also the religious left, for the Muslim communities in Europe continues to be important. Religiously motivated larger left-wing oriented constituencies of more than 3 % of the electorate are to be encountered in some European countries; many Muslims in Europe will feel much more at home in political alliances with them rather than with the often staunchly atheist secular left.

Table 10. The Strength of the Religious Left in Europe in % of the Total Population

The Catholic Left

	Religious practice	Left ... from that denominational group in % of the total population 2004 (for some countries, 2000)	DYN Left from that denominational group 2002 – 2004
SK Slovakia	Roman Catholic: observant	4,22	Xx
PL Poland	Roman Catholic: observant	4,16	-1,22
IT Italy	Roman Catholic: observant	3,2	Xx
PT Portugal	Roman Catholic: observant	2,56	0,49
IE Ireland	Roman Catholic: observant	1,28	-0,49
ES Spain	Roman Catholic: observant	1,14	-0,07
CZ Czech Republic	Roman Catholic: observant	0,93	0,36
HU Hungary	Roman Catholic: observant	0,85	Xx
AT Austria	Roman Catholic: observant	0,72	0,15
CH Switzerland	Roman Catholic: observant	0,41	0,09
IL Israel	Roman Catholic: observant	0,39	Xx
GB United Kingdom	Roman Catholic: observant	0,35	0,14
BE Belgium	Roman Catholic: observant	0,31	-0,24
LU Luxembourg	Roman Catholic: observant	0,3	-0,45
FR France	Roman Catholic: observant	0,21	Xx

Table 10. (Continued)

The Catholic Left

	Religious practice	Left … from that denominational group in % of the total population 2004 (for some countries, 2000)	DYN Left from that denominational group 2002 – 2004
SI Slovenia	Roman Catholic: observant	0,19	-0,31
DE Germany	Roman Catholic: observant	0,12	-0,14
NL Netherlands	Roman Catholic: observant	0,06	-0,03

The Protestant Left

	Religious practice	Left … from that denominational group in % of the total population 2002	DYN Left from that denominational group 2002 - 2004
CH Switzerland	Protestant: observant	0,46	0,46
SK Slovakia	Protestant: observant	0,24	xx
EE Estonia	Protestant: observant	0,2	xx
GB United Kingdom	Protestant: observant	0,18	0,07
NL Netherlands	Protestant: observant	0,17	-0,01
ES Spain	Protestant: observant	0,14	0,14
DE Germany	Protestant: observant	0,12	0,01
IT Italy	Protestant: observant	0,11	xx
NO Norway	Protestant: observant	0,11	0,06
SE Sweden	Protestant: observant	0,11	-0,06
SI Slovenia	Protestant: observant	0,1	0,1
UA Ukraine	Protestant: observant	0,08	xx
DK Denmark	Protestant: observant	0,07	0,07
BE Belgium	Protestant: observant	0,06	0,06
FI Finland	Protestant: observant	0,05	xx
GR Greece	Protestant: observant	0,05	0,05
CZ Czech Republic	Protestant: observant	0,04	-0,12

The Muslim Left[1]

	strength of the total Muslim left per cent of total population
IL Israel	9,31
FR France	1,13
BE Belgium	1,05
ES Spain	0,35
CH Switzerland	0,25
DE Germany	0,24
GB United Kingdom	0,23
NL Netherlands	0,23
AT Austria	0,15
SI Slovenia	0,1
UA Ukraine	0,08
DK Denmark	0,07
NO Norway	0,06
SE Sweden	0,05

In terms of the policy conclusions for the European policy makers, our advice is relatively simple – do everything that Muslim elites can develop in Europe. Table 10 further summarizes our results in the shape of a target scoreboard for European decision makers. Human development, i.e. fulfilling the Lisbon process, well explains (1/3) of centrist political orientation in Europe. Just these two variables, the Lisbon process, and creating or strengthening the political center will be, according to our analysis, the really decisive ones also in determining the success or failure of *"Muslim integration"* = implementing the Lisbon process in Europe. If Samuel Huntington and the development of global terrorism especially since 9/11 posed the question, certainly the development of *"Muslim Calvinism"* is the answer for Europe. The rest – i.e. Islamophobia – is based on myths and fantasies.

Table 11. Implementing Lisbon, furthering human development, creating a middle class – an international scoreboard

	UNDP HDI as a proxy for the Lisbon process	Overall, country-wide center+center left+center right political orientation
Austria	0,936	78,9
Belgium	0,945	80,4
Czech	0,874	64
Denmark	0,941	76,9
Estonia	0,853	80,1

---

[1] Religiously observing persons, selectively observing persons, and secular Muslims combined

Table 11. (Continued)

	UNDP HDI as a proxy for the Lisbon process	Overall, country-wide center+center left+center right political orientation
Finland	0,941	73,3
France	0,998	70,7
Germany	0,93	82,3
Greece	0,912	69,2
Hungary	0,862	72,8
Iceland	0,956	77,3
Ireland	0,946	85,1
Israel	0,915	48,7
Italy	0,934	71,8
Luxembourg	0,949	77,7
Netherlands	0,943	78,3
Norway	0,963	77,9
Poland	0,858	71,8
Portugal	0,904	73,8
Slovakia	0,849	69,7
Slovenia	0,904	71,9
Spain	0,928	72,2
Sweden	0,949	71,7
Switzerland	0,947	80,9
Ukraine	0,766	64
United Kingdom	0,939	85,4

Source: estimated by the author, based on the data calculations provided by Christian Bischof, Tomaz Kastrun, Karl Mueller and the author from the data of the ESS, available at *http://www.european socialsurvey.org/* .

APPENDIX

Fallzahl = n number of cases

1. Joined ESS1 and ESS2 on "satisfied with democracy"

		How satisfied with the way democracy works in country									
		ESS1					ESS2				
		0	1	2	3	Fallzahl	0	1	2	3	Fallzahl
Austria	Muslims	3,8	3,8	11,5	0,0	26,0	0,0	0,0	0,0	4,8	21
	Non Muslims	3,1	1,9	4,3	9,2	1438,0	1,1	1,3	3,3	6,7	1472
Belgium	Muslims	0,0	0,0	2,9	0,0	35,0	1,8	0,0	7,1	5,4	56
	Non Muslims	1,7	1,4	4,0	6,9	828,0	2,6	1,7	5,7	6,8	725
Switzerland	Muslims	0,0	0,0	9,1	0,0	11,0	0,0	3,6	0,0	3,6	28
	Non Muslims	0,7	0,4	1,8	3,7	1201,0	0,6	0,8	1,7	3,4	1416
Czech Repub	Muslims	0,0	0,0	0,0	0,0	0,0	0,0	0,0	0,0	0,0	0
	Non Muslims	5,1	5,4	9,0	16,1	410,0	6,9	5,1	8,1	11,8	788
Germany	Muslims	3,5	3,5	0,0	7,0	57,0	1,7	3,3	3,3	3,3	60
	Non Muslims	3,6	1,8	4,5	10,7	1511,0	3,2	2,8	6,3	8,1	1450
Denmark	Muslims	0,0	0,0	0,0	0,0	20,0	0,0	6,3	6,3	0,0	16
	Non Muslims	0,6	0,2	0,7	1,2	830,0	0,1	0,7	1,3	2,7	877
Estonia	Muslims						0,0	0,0	0,0	33,3	3
	Non Muslims						7,7	7,7	8,2	15,3	378
Spain	Muslims	14,3	0,0	14,3	14,3	7,0	0,0	0,0	0,0	9,5	21
	Non Muslims	1,5	1,1	2,9	6,4	1227,0	1,6	1,1	3,1	4,5	1141
Finland	Muslims	0,0	0,0	0,0	0,0	3,0	0,0	0,0	0,0	0,0	0
	Non Muslims	0,8	1,1	1,6	3,6	1461,0	0,0	0,0	0,0	0,0	0
France	Muslims	3,8	1,9	1,9	7,7	52,0	0,0	0,0	0,0	0,0	0
	Non Muslims	4,2	2,2	6,6	9,3	687,0	0,0	0,0	0,0	0,0	0
United Kingdc	Muslims	0,0	2,9	5,9	8,8	34,0	0,0	0,0	8,7	8,7	46
	Non Muslims	3,4	1,7	6,5	11,1	940,0	3,6	2,4	6,1	10,4	872
Greece	Muslims	1,5	1,5	1,5	3,0	66,0	0,0	0,0	0,0	0,0	34
	Non Muslims	4,0	4,3	5,2	7,3	2352,0	1,3	1,8	2,8	5,1	2098
Hungary	Muslims	0,0	0,0	0,0	0,0	0,0	0,0	0,0	0,0	0,0	0
	Non Muslims	4,9	2,7	6,3	11,4	956,0	0,0	0,0	0,0	0,0	0
Ireland	Muslims	0,0	0,0	0,0	0,0	2,0	0,0	0,0	0,0	0,0	0
	Non Muslims	5,7	3,9	6,9	8,8	1551,0	2,1	2,0	3,4	5,7	1867
Iceland	Muslims						0,0	0,0	0,0	0,0	0
	Non Muslims						3,1	0,8	2,7	9,7	257
Israel	Muslims	22,3	7,8	10,0	9,2	359,0					
	Non Muslims	7,0	2,6	6,6	9,5	1446,0					
Italy	Muslims	0,0	0,0	0,0	0,0	1,0					
	Non Muslims	4,6	2,5	5,5	9,8	869,0					
Luxembourg	Muslims	4,2	0,0	4,2	12,5	24,0	0,0	0,0	4,8	0,0	21
	Non Muslims	1,2	0,5	1,1	3,1	1001,0	1,3	0,6	1,0	3,0	1023
Netherlands	Muslims	5,1	0,0	7,7	12,8	39,0	3,6	7,1	10,7	7,1	28
	Non Muslims	0,6	1,1	1,0	4,7	960,0	1,0	1,1	4,1	5,3	809
Norway	Muslims	5,0	0,0	0,0	10,0	20,0	0,0	0,0	0,0	0,0	22
	Non Muslims	0,6	0,7	1,8	4,4	994,0	0,9	1,1	1,6	6,4	855
Poland	Muslims	0,0	0,0	0,0	0,0	0,0	0,0	0,0	0,0	0,0	1
	Non Muslims	7,8	5,6	10,3	16,0	1811,0	10,8	7,1	12,5	15,4	1483
Portugal	Muslims	0,0	0,0	0,0	0,0	1,0	0,0	0,0	0,0	0,0	1
	Non Muslims	5,5	3,7	7,7	11,5	1137,0	7,4	12,8	17,2	18,3	1670
Sweden	Muslims	0,0	0,0	0,0	4,2	24,0	7,1	0,0	0,0	0,0	14
	Non Muslims	1,3	0,9	2,2	5,8	534,0	2,1	0,9	4,5	8,1	581
Slovenia	Muslims	11,1	0,0	16,7	0,0	18,0	0,0	0,0	42,9	0,0	7
	Non Muslims	6,4	4,6	10,2	15,0	714,0	5,6	2,8	10,3	12,6	708
Slovakia	Muslims						0,0	0,0	0,0	100,0	2
	Non Muslims						12,2	7,5	11,7	13,8	1065
Ukraine	Muslims						30,0	10,0	0,0	0,0	10
	Non Muslims						13,9	6,2	7,4	12,7	1187

2. Joined ESS1 and ESS2 on "income"

		Feeling about household's income nowadays ESS1					Trust in country's parliament ESS2				
		Living comfortably on present income	Coping on present income	Difficult on present income	Very difficult on present income	Fallzahl	Living comfortably on present income	Coping on present income	Difficult on present income	Very difficult on present income	Fallzahl
Austria	Muslims	3,3	60,0	20,0	16,7	30	14,0	46,4	17,9	20,0	29
	Non Muslims	30,6	51,1	13,6	4,7	1478	39,2	48,9	9,3	2,7	1506
Belgium	Muslims	20,6	52,9	23,5	2,9	34	17,2	36,2	37,9	8,6	58
	Non Muslims	41,6	42,9	12,4	3,0	855	34,2	43,8	16,5	5,4	739
Switzerland	Muslims	30,8	61,5	0,0	7,7	13	6,7	36,7	43,3	13,3	30
	Non Muslims	52,2	39,5	7,1	1,1	1222	48,3	39,6	9,8	2,3	1462
Czech Repub	Muslims	0,0	0,0	0,0	0,0	0	0,0	0,0	0,0	0,0	0
	Non Muslims	7,9	51,7	32,0	8,4	441	7,3	43,4	34,0	15,3	779
Germany	Muslims	8,8	63,2	26,3	1,8	57	6,3	46,0	30,2	17,5	63
	Non Muslims	31,1	58,2	9,0	1,7	1514	29,9	55,4	12,3	2,5	1474
Denmark	Muslims	28,6	52,4	19,0	0,0	21	18,8	56,3	6,3	18,8	16
	Non Muslims	67,9	27,1	4,0	1,1	835	65,6	30,5	3,5	0,4	897
Estonia	Muslims						0,0	33,3	66,7	0,0	3
	Non Muslims						6,1	41,6	34,8	17,4	442
Spain	Muslims	0,0	33,3	22,2	44,4	9	0,0	36,0	48,0	16,0	25
	Non Muslims	28,7	49,5	17,9	3,9	1305	36,4	45,7	15,1	2,9	1176
Finland	Muslims	0,0	66,7	33,3	0,0	3	0,0	0,0	0,0	0,0	0
	Non Muslims	21,1	65,5	9,8	3,6	1491	0,0	0,0	0,0	0,0	0
France	Muslims	2,0	18,4	61,2	18,4	49	0,0	0,0	0,0	0,0	0
	Non Muslims	8,4	47,5	35,5	8,5	692	0,0	0,0	0,0	0,0	0
United Kingdo	Muslims	11,1	61,1	25,0	2,8	36	25,0	47,9	18,8	8,3	48
	Non Muslims	43,1	44,7	10,9	1,3	973	38,8	44,1	12,8	4,2	904
Greece	Muslims	2,8	16,9	39,4	40,8	71	2,9	14,3	45,7	37,1	35
	Non Muslims	10,8	37,3	35,6	16,3	2393	9,2	40,4	36,3	14,1	2127
Hungary	Muslims	0,0	0,0	0,0	0,0	0	0,0	0,0	0,0	0,0	0
	Non Muslims	5,4	45,3	37,0	12,3	1052	0,0	0,0	0,0	0,0	0
Ireland	Muslims	0,0	100,0	0,0	0,0	2	0,0	0,0	0,0	0,0	0
	Non Muslims	37,3	47,1	12,3	3,4	1661	48,4	41,1	8,8	1,7	1974
Iceland	Muslims						0,0	0,0	0,0	0,0	0
	Non Muslims						58,6	33,5	4,2	3,8	263
Israel	Muslims	18,1	34,5	28,5	18,9	365					
	Non Muslims	17,8	42,7	26,2	13,3	1456					
Italy	Muslims	0,0	100,0	0,0	0,0	1					
	Non Muslims	33,5	49,5	14,7	2,3	907					
Luxembourg	Muslims	30,8	30,8	19,2	19,2	26	4,3	47,8	30,4	17,4	23
	Non Muslims	54,6	35,7	8,6	1,1	1099	52,2	36,5	8,8	2,5	1106
Netherlands	Muslims	20,5	48,7	20,5	10,3	39	14,3	32,1	39,3	14,3	28
	Non Muslims	51,9	38,5	8,4	1,2	980	44,1	43,0	10,4	2,5	835
Norway	Muslims	10,0	55,0	25,0	10,0	20	45,5	27,3	27,3	0,0	22
	Non Muslims	52,7	39,6	6,5	1,2	1007	52,9	38,0	6,4	2,8	859
Poland	Muslims	0,0	0,0	0,0	0,0	0	0,0	100,0	0,0	0,0	1
	Non Muslims	4,6	49,7	39,8	5,9	1935	4,9	54,1	35,8	5,2	1563
Portugal	Muslims	0,0	100,0	0,0	0,0	1	0,0	0,0	100,0	0,0	1
	Non Muslims	7,9	51,0	30,5	10,6	1240	7,8	52,2	29,2	10,8	1751
Sweden	Muslims	26,1	47,8	17,4	8,7	23	21,4	50,0	14,3	14,3	14
	Non Muslims	53,5	37,8	7,3	1,4	561	56,1	35,2	7,3	1,3	599
Slovenia	Muslims	15,8	63,2	15,8	5,3	19	40,0	50,0	10,0	0,0	10
	Non Muslims	33,2	49,4	14,2	3,2	741	38,4	47,5	11,4	2,7	747
Slovakia	Muslims						0,0	50,0	50,0	0,0	2
	Non Muslims						5,0	40,2	35,8	19,0	1097
Ukraine	Muslims						0,0	20,0	50,0	30,0	10
	Non Muslims						1,0	19,5	46,8	32,7	1386

Source: calculated by Christian Bischof, Tomaz Kastrun, Karl Mueller and the author from the data of the ESS, available at http://www.europeansocialsurvey.org/

Endnotes on Data and Results:

1. Data were downloaded on 18.6.2006 from www.europeansocialsurvey.com. ESS1 (5.1edt) and ESS2 (2.0edt).

2. Variables used: TRSTPRL, TRSTLGL, TRSTPLC, TRSTPLT, STFDEM, RIGDNM* and HINCFEL.

Trust variables (TRSTPRL, TRSTLGL, TRSTPLC and TRSTPLT) and STFDEM have 11 items scales: 0 – No trust at all, 1 – 1, …, 9 – 9, 10 – Complete trust.

Rigdnm was made a dummy variable with the same the pattern as shown in 3.

HIMCFEL has 4 items scale: 1 – Living comfortably on present income,

2 – Coping on present income,

3 – Finding it difficult on present income,

4 – Finding it very difficult on present income.

3. Variable RELIGION is recoded RigDnm* variable with the following procedure: item 6 = Muslims, Items 1+2+3+4+5+7+8 = Non Muslims.

4. All the results shown are represented in percentage (%).

In section 1 (on trust) + 2 (satisfied with democracy) values are the percentage (%) presenting *only first four values on 11-items scales* and are prepared to have comparability. Row total of the whole 11-items scale is 100%.

In section 3 (on income) the percentage (%) are row totals (100%) for each country on Muslim|NonMuslim.

3. RELIGIOUS PRACTICE VERSUS SECULARISM IN EUROPE AND IN ISRAEL

Country	Religious practice		% of total pop 2002	% of total pop 2004	dyn % total pop
AT Austria	Muslim: weekly or more frequent	AT	0,2	0,2	-0,1
AT Austria	Orthodox: weekly or more frequent	AT	0,2	0,0	-0,2
AT Austria	Muslim: less frequent than every week	AT	0,3	0,7	0,4
AT Austria	Protestant: weekly or more frequent	AT	0,3	0,5	0,2
AT Austria	Orthodox: less frequent than every week	AT	0,7	0,4	-0,3
AT Austria	Protestant: less frequent than every week	AT	2,6	2,5	-0,1
AT Austria	Roman Catholic: weekly or more frequent	AT	15,2	12,8	-2,4
AT Austria	Roman Catholic: less frequent than every week	AT	37,0	41,6	4,5
BE Belgium	Orthodox: weekly or more frequent	BE	0,0	0,0	0,0
BE Belgium	Protestant: weekly or more frequent	BE	0,1	0,2	0,2
BE Belgium	Orthodox: less frequent than every week	BE	0,1	0,1	-0,1
BE Belgium	Muslim: weekly or more frequent	BE	0,2	0,7	0,4
BE Belgium	Protestant: less frequent than every week	BE	0,4	0,3	-0,1
BE Belgium	Muslim: less frequent than every week	BE	1,0	1,9	0,9
BE Belgium	Roman Catholic: weekly or more frequent	BE	9,4	7,2	-2,3
BE Belgium	Roman Catholic: less frequent than every week	BE	24,2	20,6	-3,6

(Continued)

Country	Religious practice		% of total pop 2002	% of total pop 2004	dyn % total pop
CH Switzerland	Orthodox: weekly or more frequent	CH	0,0	0,1	0,1
CH Switzerland	Muslim: less frequent than every week	CH	0,2	0,6	0,5
CH Switzerland	Muslim: weekly or more frequent	CH	0,3	0,3	0,0
CH Switzerland	Orthodox: less frequent than every week	CH	0,3	0,8	0,5
CH Switzerland	Protestant: weekly or more frequent	CH	1,6	4,1	2,4
CH Switzerland	Roman Catholic: weekly or more frequent	CH	5,8	6,7	0,9
CH Switzerland	Protestant: less frequent than every week	CH	20,0	24,7	4,8
CH Switzerland	Roman Catholic: less frequent than every week	CH	21,3	22,4	1,1
CZ Czech Republic	Muslim: less frequent than every week	CZ	0,0	0,0	0,0
CZ Czech Republic	Muslim: weekly or more frequent	CZ	0,0	0,0	0,0
CZ Czech Republic	Orthodox: less frequent than every week	CZ	0,0	0,1	0,1
CZ Czech Republic	Orthodox: weekly or more frequent	CZ	0,0	0,1	0,1
CZ Czech Republic	Protestant: weekly or more frequent	CZ	0,7	0,4	-0,3
CZ Czech Republic	Protestant: less frequent than every week	CZ	2,0	1,7	-0,4
CZ Czech Republic	Roman Catholic: weekly or more frequent	CZ	7,2	6,4	-0,8
CZ Czech Republic	Roman Catholic: less frequent than every week	CZ	16,4	15,2	-1,1
DE Germany	Orthodox: weekly or more frequent	DE	0,1	0,0	0,0
DE Germany	Muslim: weekly or more frequent	DE	0,3	0,6	0,4
DE Germany	Orthodox: less frequent than every week	DE	0,4	0,6	0,1
DE Germany	Muslim: less frequent than every week	DE	1,0	0,8	-0,1
DE Germany	Protestant: weekly or more frequent	DE	1,7	2,0	0,3
DE Germany	Roman Catholic: weekly or more frequent	DE	4,5	4,5	0,0
DE Germany	Roman Catholic: less frequent than every week	DE	13,4	14,8	1,5
DE Germany	Protestant: less frequent than every week	DE	23,6	19,8	-3,8
DK Denmark	Orthodox: weekly or more frequent	DK	0,0	0,0	0,0
DK Denmark	Roman Catholic: weekly or more frequent	DK	0,1	0,1	0,0
DK Denmark	Muslim: weekly or more frequent	DK	0,1	0,3	0,1

(Continued)

Country	Religious practice		% of total pop 2002	% of total pop 2004	dyn % total pop
DK Denmark	Roman Catholic: less frequent than every week	DK	0,4	0,9	0,4
DK Denmark	Muslim: less frequent than every week	DK	0,7	0,5	-0,2
DK Denmark	Protestant: weekly or more frequent	DK	1,7	2,2	0,5
DK Denmark	Protestant: less frequent than every week	DK	38,2	44,0	5,8
EE Estonia	Muslim: less frequent than every week	EE		0,1	
EE Estonia	Muslim: weekly or more frequent	EE		0,0	
EE Estonia	Orthodox: less frequent than every week	EE		8,9	
EE Estonia	Orthodox: weekly or more frequent	EE		1,0	
EE Estonia	Protestant: less frequent than every week	EE		6,5	
EE Estonia	Protestant: weekly or more frequent	EE		1,9	
EE Estonia	Roman Catholic: less frequent than every week	EE		0,6	
EE Estonia	Roman Catholic: weekly or more frequent	EE		0,1	
ES Spain	Muslim: less frequent than every week	ES	0,0	0,4	0,4
ES Spain	Orthodox: less frequent than every week	ES	0,0	0,2	0,2
ES Spain	Orthodox: weekly or more frequent	ES	0,0	0,1	0,1
ES Spain	Protestant: less frequent than every week	ES	0,1	0,1	0,0
ES Spain	Muslim: weekly or more frequent	ES	0,2	0,1	-0,1
ES Spain	Protestant: weekly or more frequent	ES	0,2	0,4	0,1
ES Spain	Roman Catholic: weekly or more frequent	ES	19,2	16,2	-3,0
ES Spain	Roman Catholic: less frequent than every week	ES	38,4	34,7	-3,7
FI Finland	Muslim: weekly or more frequent	FI	0,0		
FI Finland	Roman Catholic: weekly or more frequent	FI	0,0		
FI Finland	Muslim: less frequent than every week	FI	0,1		
FI Finland	Orthodox: weekly or more frequent	FI	0,1		
FI Finland	Roman Catholic: less frequent than every week	FI	0,1		
FI Finland	Orthodox: less frequent than every week	FI	0,9		
FI Finland	Protestant: weekly or more frequent	FI	3,6		

(Continued)

Country	Religious practice		% of total pop 2002	% of total pop 2004	dyn % total pop
FI Finland	Protestant: less frequent than every week	FI	57,8		
FR France	Orthodox: weekly or more frequent	FR	0,0		
FR France	Orthodox: less frequent than every week	FR	0,1		
FR France	Protestant: weekly or more frequent	FR	0,2		
FR France	Muslim: weekly or more frequent	FR	0,3		
FR France	Protestant: less frequent than every week	FR	0,9		
FR France	Muslim: less frequent than every week	FR	2,4		
FR France	Roman Catholic: weekly or more frequent	FR	6,6		
FR France	Roman Catholic: less frequent than every week	FR	25,3		
GB United Kingdom	Orthodox: weekly or more frequent	GB	0,0	0,1	0,1
GB United Kingdom	Orthodox: less frequent than every week	GB	0,1	0,1	0,1
GB United Kingdom	Muslim: weekly or more frequent	GB	0,5	0,9	0,5
GB United Kingdom	Muslim: less frequent than every week	GB	0,6	1,0	0,3
GB United Kingdom	Roman Catholic: less frequent than every week	GB	3,6	4,4	0,8
GB United Kingdom	Roman Catholic: weekly or more frequent	GB	4,2	4,3	0,1
GB United Kingdom	Protestant: weekly or more frequent	GB	6,1	5,4	-0,8
GB United Kingdom	Protestant: less frequent than every week	GB	18,3	12,7	-5,6
GR Greece	Protestant: weekly or more frequent	GR	0,1	0,1	0,0
GR Greece	Roman Catholic: less frequent than every week	GR	0,1	0,6	0,5
GR Greece	Roman Catholic: weekly or more frequent	GR	0,1	0,2	0,1
GR Greece	Protestant: less frequent than every week	GR	0,3	0,1	-0,1
GR Greece	Muslim: weekly or more frequent	GR	0,4	0,5	0,1
GR Greece	Muslim: less frequent than every week	GR	1,0	0,3	-0,7
GR Greece	Orthodox: weekly or more frequent	GR	24,6	23,4	-1,2
GR Greece	Orthodox: less frequent than every week	GR	66,6	63,5	-3,1
HU Hungary	Muslim: less frequent than every week	HU	0,0		
HU Hungary	Muslim: weekly or more frequent	HU	0,0		

(Continued)

Country	Religious practice		% of total pop 2002	% of total pop 2004	dyn % total pop
HU Hungary	Orthodox: weekly or more frequent	HU	0,0		
HU Hungary	Orthodox: less frequent than every week	HU	0,1		
HU Hungary	Protestant: weekly or more frequent	HU	1,6		
HU Hungary	Roman Catholic: weekly or more frequent	HU	9,1		
HU Hungary	Protestant: less frequent than every week	HU	11,4		
HU Hungary	Roman Catholic: less frequent than every week	HU	28,5		
IE Ireland	Orthodox: less frequent than every week	IE	0,0	0,0	0,0
IE Ireland	Orthodox: weekly or more frequent	IE	0,0	0,0	0,0
IE Ireland	Muslim: less frequent than every week	IE	0,1	0,0	-0,1
IE Ireland	Muslim: weekly or more frequent	IE	0,1	0,0	-0,1
IE Ireland	Protestant: less frequent than every week	IE	1,5	1,6	0,1
IE Ireland	Protestant: weekly or more frequent	IE	1,7	1,4	-0,3
IE Ireland	Roman Catholic: less frequent than every week	IE	26,4	25,8	-0,6
IE Ireland	Roman Catholic: weekly or more frequent	IE	49,0	55,4	6,5
IL Israel	Orthodox: less frequent than every week	IL	0,0		
IL Israel	Orthodox: weekly or more frequent	IL	0,0		
IL Israel	Protestant: less frequent than every week	IL	0,0		
IL Israel	Protestant: weekly or more frequent	IL	0,0		
IL Israel	Roman Catholic: weekly or more frequent	IL	0,7		
IL Israel	Roman Catholic: less frequent than every week	IL	2,6		
IL Israel	Muslim: weekly or more frequent	IL	4,3		
IL Israel	Muslim: less frequent than every week	IL	8,7		
IS Iceland	Muslim: less frequent than every week	IS		0,0	
IS Iceland	Muslim: weekly or more frequent	IS		0,0	
IS Iceland	Orthodox: less frequent than every week	IS		0,0	
IS Iceland	Orthodox: weekly or more frequent	IS		0,0	
IS Iceland	Protestant: less frequent than every week	IS		30,8	

(Continued)

Country	Religious practice		% of total pop 2002	% of total pop 2004	dyn % total pop
IS Iceland	Protestant: weekly or more frequent	IS		2,3	
IS Iceland	Roman Catholic: less frequent than every week	IS		0,0	
IS Iceland	Roman Catholic: weekly or more frequent	IS		0,0	
IT Italy	Muslim: less frequent than every week	IT	0,0		
IT Italy	Muslim: weekly or more frequent	IT	0,0		
IT Italy	Orthodox: less frequent than every week	IT	0,0		
IT Italy	Orthodox: weekly or more frequent	IT	0,0		
IT Italy	Protestant: less frequent than every week	IT	0,3		
IT Italy	Protestant: weekly or more frequent	IT	0,4		
IT Italy	Roman Catholic: weekly or more frequent	IT	27,6		
IT Italy	Roman Catholic: less frequent than every week	IT	41,2		
LU Luxembourg	Protestant: weekly or more frequent	LU	0,0	0,0	0,0
LU Luxembourg	Muslim: weekly or more frequent	LU	0,1	0,0	-0,1
LU Luxembourg	Orthodox: less frequent than every week	LU	0,2	0,1	-0,1
LU Luxembourg	Orthodox: weekly or more frequent	LU	0,2	0,1	-0,1
LU Luxembourg	Muslim: less frequent than every week	LU	0,3	0,2	0,0
LU Luxembourg	Protestant: less frequent than every week	LU	0,6	0,6	0,0
LU Luxembourg	Roman Catholic: weekly or more frequent	LU	11,1	9,7	-1,4
LU Luxembourg	Roman Catholic: less frequent than every week	LU	27,0	33,1	6,1
NL Netherlands	Orthodox: weekly or more frequent	NL	0,0	0,0	0,0
NL Netherlands	Orthodox: less frequent than every week	NL	0,1	0,1	0,0
NL Netherlands	Muslim: weekly or more frequent	NL	0,4	0,2	-0,2
NL Netherlands	Muslim: less frequent than every week	NL	0,8	0,6	-0,2
NL Netherlands	Roman Catholic: weekly or more frequent	NL	3,2	3,7	0,5
NL Netherlands	Protestant: weekly or more frequent	NL	6,8	7,4	0,5
NL Netherlands	Protestant: less frequent than every week	NL	6,9	7,1	0,2
NL Netherlands	Roman Catholic: less frequent than every week	NL	13,8	14,8	1,0

(Continued)

Country	Religious practice		% of total pop 2002	% of total pop 2004	dyn % total pop
NO Norway	Orthodox: weekly or more frequent	NO	0,0	0,1	0,1
NO Norway	Roman Catholic: weekly or more frequent	NO	0,1	0,2	0,2
NO Norway	Muslim: weekly or more frequent	NO	0,1	0,3	0,2
NO Norway	Orthodox: less frequent than every week	NO	0,2	0,3	0,1
NO Norway	Roman Catholic: less frequent than every week	NO	0,4	0,6	0,3
NO Norway	Muslim: less frequent than every week	NO	0,5	0,6	0,1
NO Norway	Protestant: weekly or more frequent	NO	2,8	2,9	0,1
NO Norway	Protestant: less frequent than every week	NO	33,1	31,2	-1,9
PL Poland	Muslim: less frequent than every week	PL	0,0	0,1	0,1
PL Poland	Muslim: weekly or more frequent	PL	0,0	0,0	0,0
PL Poland	Protestant: less frequent than every week	PL	0,1	0,1	0,0
PL Poland	Protestant: weekly or more frequent	PL	0,1	0,1	0,0
PL Poland	Orthodox: weekly or more frequent	PL	0,2	0,0	-0,2
PL Poland	Orthodox: less frequent than every week	PL	0,5	0,6	0,1
PL Poland	Roman Catholic: less frequent than every week	PL	34,9	33,1	-1,8
PL Poland	Roman Catholic: weekly or more frequent	PL	53,8	56,2	2,4
PT Portugal	Muslim: less frequent than every week	PT	0,0	0,0	0,0
PT Portugal	Muslim: weekly or more frequent	PT	0,0	0,1	0,1
PT Portugal	Orthodox: less frequent than every week	PT	0,0	0,0	0,0
PT Portugal	Orthodox: weekly or more frequent	PT	0,0	0,0	0,0
PT Portugal	Protestant: less frequent than every week	PT	0,0	0,1	0,1
PT Portugal	Protestant: weekly or more frequent	PT	0,7	0,4	-0,4
PT Portugal	Roman Catholic: weekly or more frequent	PT	26,2	26,1	0,0
PT Portugal	Roman Catholic: less frequent than every week	PT	42,6	45,0	2,4
SE Sweden	Orthodox: weekly or more frequent	SE	0,0	0,1	0,1
SE Sweden	Roman Catholic: weekly or more frequent	SE	0,0	0,2	0,2
SE Sweden	Muslim: weekly or more frequent	SE	0,1	0,0	-0,1

(Continued)

Country	Religious practice		% of total pop 2002	% of total pop 2004	dyn % total pop
SE Sweden	Orthodox: less frequent than every week	SE	0,4	0,3	-0,2
SE Sweden	Roman Catholic: less frequent than every week	SE	0,8	0,8	0,0
SE Sweden	Muslim: less frequent than every week	SE	0,9	0,3	-0,6
SE Sweden	Protestant: weekly or more frequent	SE	3,1	2,2	-0,9
SE Sweden	Protestant: less frequent than every week	SE	17,5	20,3	2,8
SI Slovenia	Muslim: weekly or more frequent	SI	0,1	0,1	0,0
SI Slovenia	Orthodox: weekly or more frequent	SI	0,1	0,2	0,1
SI Slovenia	Protestant: weekly or more frequent	SI	0,1	0,2	0,1
SI Slovenia	Protestant: less frequent than every week	SI	0,3	0,7	0,3
SI Slovenia	Muslim: less frequent than every week	SI	0,5	0,4	-0,1
SI Slovenia	Orthodox: less frequent than every week	SI	0,9	0,6	-0,3
SI Slovenia	Roman Catholic: weekly or more frequent	SI	15,8	8,7	-7,1
SI Slovenia	Roman Catholic: less frequent than every week	SI	26,4	27,9	1,6
SK Slovakia	Muslim: less frequent than every week	SK		0,1	
SK Slovakia	Muslim: weekly or more frequent	SK		0,1	
SK Slovakia	Orthodox: less frequent than every week	SK		0,6	
SK Slovakia	Orthodox: weekly or more frequent	SK		0,4	
SK Slovakia	Protestant: less frequent than every week	SK		4,5	
SK Slovakia	Protestant: weekly or more frequent	SK		1,6	
SK Slovakia	Roman Catholic: less frequent than every week	SK		27,7	
SK Slovakia	Roman Catholic: weekly or more frequent	SK		27,0	
UA Ukraine	Muslim: less frequent than every week	UA		0,2	
UA Ukraine	Muslim: weekly or more frequent	UA		0,0	
UA Ukraine	Orthodox: less frequent than every week	UA		46,6	
UA Ukraine	Orthodox: weekly or more frequent	UA		6,3	
UA Ukraine	Protestant: less frequent than every week	UA		0,2	
UA Ukraine	Protestant: weekly or more frequent	UA		1,3	

(Continued)

Country	Religious practice		% of total pop 2002	% of total pop 2004	dyn % total pop
UA Ukraine	Roman Catholic: less frequent than every week	UA		6,3	
UA Ukraine	Roman Catholic: weekly or more frequent	UA		4,1	

4. ESS RESULTS ON RELIGIOUS PRACTICE AND PERCENTAGES OF EACH DENOMINATIONAL/SOCIOLOGICAL GROUP POSITIONING ITSELF ON THE LEFT/RIGHT SCALE AND NUMBERS OF OBSERVATIONS IN THE ESS ANALYSES – EUROPE AND ISRAEL

	religious practice	left right scale ESS 1 2002						ESS 2 2004						
		left	moderate left	center	moderate right	right	n	left	moderate left	center	moderate right	right	n	
AT Austria	without denomination	22,0	26,7	32,5	13,4	5,4	610	24,5	25,7	35,6	9,3	4,9	57	AT
	Roman Catholic: weekly or more frequent	3,7	16,5	40,7	27,9	11,1	297	5,6	14,1	42,2	25,7	12,4	24	AT
	Roman Catholic: less frequent than every week	8,4	23,3	45,4	17,5	5,4	722	10,4	22,4	43,5	16,9	6,8	8	AT
	Roman Catholic: never	13,1	20,8	37,7	21,5	6,9	130	10,8	21,5	50,0	14,6	3,1	1	AT
	Protestant: weekly or more frequent	0,0	33,3	50,0	16,7	0,0	6	0,0	0,0	55,6	33,3	11,1	9	AT
	Protestant: less frequent than every week	20,0	20,0	36,0	20,0	4,0	50	8,3	33,3	33,3	20,8	4,2	4	AT
	Protestant: never	0,0	20,0	40,0	40,0	0,0	10	0,0	16,7	66,7	16,7	0,0	6	AT
	Orthodox: weekly or more frequent	25,0	25,0	50,0	0,0	0,0	4	0,0	0,0	0,0	0,0	0,0	0	AT
	Orthodox: less frequent than every week	7,7	38,5	46,2	7,7	0,0	13	25,0	25,0	37,5	12,5	0,0		AT

	religious practice	left	moderate left	center	moderate right	right	n	left	moderate left	center	moderate right	right	n	
	Orthodox: never	0,0	0,0	66,7	33,3	0,0	3	0,0	100,0	0,0	0,0	0,0	1	AT
	Muslim: weekly or more frequent	50,0	0,0	50,0	0,0	0,0	4	33,3	33,3	0,0	33,3	0,0	3	AT
	Muslim: less frequent than every week	20,0	40,0	20,0	20,0	0,0	5	7,7	30,8	61,5	0,0	0,0	13	AT
	Muslim: never	14,3	14,3	28,6	28,6	14,3	7	20,0	0,0	80,0	0,0	0,0	5	AT
	Total population	**13,2**	**23,4**	**39,3**	**17,7**	**6,3**	**1950**	**14,5**	**22,4**	**41,1**	**15,4**	**6,6**	**1947**	**AT**
BE Belgium	without denomination	16,0	23,9	36,1	16,4	7,5	848	13,1	24,4	37,0	19,2	6,3	890	BE
	Roman Catholic: weekly or more frequent	5,8	11,7	42,9	19,5	20,1	154	4,3	17,4	45,2	23,5	9,6	115	BE
	religious practice	left	moderate left	center	moderate right	right	n	left	moderate left	center	moderate right	right		
	Roman Catholic: less frequent than every week	7,3	18,9	39,4	27,5	6,8	396	7,8	17,5	34,0	29,2	11,4	332	BE
	Roman Catholic: never	9,2	19,0	39,4	21,8	10,6	142	8,1	20,5	35,7	25,4	10,3	185	BE
	Protestant: weekly or more frequent	0,0	0,0	0,0	100,0	0,0	1	25,0	0,0	25,0	50,0	0,0	4	BE
	Protestant: less frequent than every week	0,0	16,7	50,0	33,3	0,0	6	0,0	60,0	0,0	40,0	0,0	5	BE
	Protestant: never	0,0	0,0	0,0	100,0	0,0	1	0,0	0,0	100,0	0,0	0,0	1	BE

(Continued)

	religious practice	left	moderate left	center	moderate right	right	n	left	moderate left	center	moderate right	right	n	
	Orthodox: weekly or more frequent	0,0	0,0	0,0	0,0	0,0	0	0,0	0,0	0,0	0,0	0,0	0	BE
	Orthodox: less frequent than every week	0,0	50,0	0,0	50,0	0,0	2	0,0	0,0	100,0	0,0	0,0	1	BE
	Orthodox: never	0,0	0,0	0,0	0,0	0,0	0	0,0	0,0	0,0	0,0	0,0	0	BE
	Muslim: weekly or more frequent	25,0	0,0	75,0	0,0	0,0	4	18,2	27,3	36,4	9,1	9,1	11	BE
	Muslim: less frequent than every week	25,0	18,8	31,3	12,5	12,5	16	36,7	16,7	30,0	6,7	10,0	30	BE
	Muslim: never	37,5	12,5	37,5	0,0	12,5	8	50,0	12,5	25,0	12,5	0,0	8	BE
	Total population	**12,2**	**20,8**	**38,2**	**19,8**	**9,0**	**1633**	**11,4**	**21,7**	**36,6**	**22,1**	**8,1**	**1608**	**BE**
CH Switzerland	without denomination	16,3	25,7	31,7	19,2	7,0	712	13,4	28,0	31,6	18,7	8,3	55	CH
	Roman Catholic: weekly or more frequent	5,5	16,4	40,0	22,7	15,5	110	6,1	18,2	38,6	22,7	14,4	13	CH
	Roman Catholic: less frequent than every week	6,3	24,8	37,0	25,3	6,8	400	6,4	18,9	41,2	21,9	11,6	49	CH
	Roman Catholic: never	6,9	19,0	39,7	27,6	6,9	58	11,1	22,2	40,7	18,5	7,4	54	CH
	Protestant: weekly or more frequent	0,0	32,3	32,3	25,8	9,7	31	11,3	17,5	36,3	23,8	11,3	80	CH

(Continued)

	religious practice	left	moderate left	center	moderate right	right	N	left	moderate left	center	moderate right	right	n	
	Protestant: less frequent than every week	5,3	22,9	35,6	25,5	10,6	376	6,2	19,8	36,0	27,6	10,5	486	CH
	Protestant: never	9,1	36,4	24,7	22,1	7,8	77	4,8	30,1	28,9	25,3	10,8	83	CH
	Orthodox: weekly or more frequent	0,0	0,0	0,0	0,0	0,0	0	0,0	0,0	0,0	100,0	0,0	1	CH
	religious practice	left	moderate left	center	moderate right	right	n	left	moderate left	center	moderate right	right	n	
	Orthodox: less frequent than every week	0,0	0,0	66,7	33,3	0,0	6	12,5	18,8	31,3	25,0	12,5	16	CH
	Orthodox: never	100,0	0,0	0,0	0,0	0,0	1	0,0	0,0	100,0	0,0	0,0	1	CH
	Muslim: weekly or more frequent	40,0	0,0	40,0	20,0	0,0	5	20,0	20,0	40,0	0,0	20,0	5	CH
	Muslim: less frequent than every week	0,0	33,3	33,3	0,0	33,3	3	8,3	16,7	58,3	16,7	0,0	12	CH
	Muslim: never	0,0	0,0	0,0	0,0	100,0	1	0,0	28,6	28,6	0,0	0,0	7	CH
	Total population	**10,3**	**24,7**	**34,1**	**22,8**	**8,2**	**1881**	**9,0**	**22,7**	**35,9**	**22,3**	**10,1**	**1964**	**CH**
CZ Czech Republic	without denomination	10,4	20,3	28,6	17,4	23,3	811	13,4	16,8	26,2	20,1	23,5	1712	CZ
	Roman Catholic: weekly or more frequent	8,0	19,3	31,8	23,9	17,0	88	14,5	12,6	26,4	26,4	20,1	159	CZ

(Continued)

religious practice	left	moderate left	center	moderate right	right	n	left	moderate left	center	moderate right	right	n	CZ
Roman Catholic: less frequent than every week	8,5	20,0	31,0	22,0	18,5	200	10,6	19,1	27,1	18,8	24,4	377	CZ
Roman Catholic: never	14,5	14,5	29,1	14,5	27,3	55	11,9	19,0	44,0	10,7	14,3	84	CZ
Protestant: weekly or more frequent	22,2	11,1	22,2	22,2	22,2	9	9,1	0,0	18,2	27,3	45,5	11	CZ
Protestant: less frequent than every week	24,0	24,0	8,0	24,0	20,0	25	12,2	22,0	22,0	17,1	26,8	41	CZ
Protestant: never	10,0	40,0	10,0	30,0	10,0	10	37,5	18,8	18,8	6,3	18,8	16	CZ
Orthodox: weekly or more frequent	0,0	0,0	0,0	0,0	0,0	0	33,3	0,0	0,0	66,7	0,0	3	CZ
Orthodox: less frequent than every week	0,0	0,0	0,0	0,0	0,0	0	0,0	50,0	0,0	50,0	0,0	2	CZ
Orthodox: never	0,0	0,0	0,0	0,0	0,0	0	0,0	0,0	0,0	100,0	0,0	1	CZ
Muslim: weekly or more frequent	0,0	0,0	0,0	0,0	0,0	0	0,0	0,0	0,0	0,0	0,0	0	CZ
Muslim: less frequent than every week	0,0	0,0	0,0	0,0	0,0	0	0,0	0,0	0,0	0,0	0,0	0	CZ
Muslim: never	0,0	0,0	0,0	0,0	0,0	0	0,0	0,0	0,0	0,0	0,0	0	CZ
Total population	**10,8**	**20,0**	**28,6**	**18,7**	**21,9**	**1223**	**13,0**	**17,0**	**27,1**	**20,0**	**22,9**	**2=5**	**CZ**

(Continued)

	religious practice	left	moderate left	center	moderate right	right	n	left	moderate left	center	moderate right	right	n	
DE Germany	without denomination	15,7	30,2	36,3	12,8	5,1	1237	19,1	28,2	37,9	10,6	4,2	1194	DE
	Roman Catholic: weekly or more frequent	5,7	18,9	36,9	23,8	14,8	122	2,6	23,1	44,4	21,4	8,5	117	DE
	Roman Catholic: less frequent than every week	5,0	26,2	45,0	17,1	6,6	362	6,0	29,9	41,9	18,5	3,6	384	DE
	Roman Catholic: never	16,3	20,4	44,9	14,3	4,1	49	11,3	22,5	45,0	12,5	8,8	80	DE
	Protestant: weekly or more frequent	6,4	27,7	34,0	23,4	8,5	47	5,8	21,2	48,1	19,2	5,8	52	DE
	Protestant: less frequent than every week	8,4	27,8	36,6	19,5	7,7	640	6,2	29,8	38,0	20,9	5,1	513	DE
	Protestant: never	14,0	28,9	40,4	8,8	7,9	114	14,2	26,7	33,3	14,2	11,7	120	DE
	Orthodox: weekly or more frequent	0,0	0,0	100,0	0,0	0,0	2	0,0	0,0	0,0	0,0	100,0	1	DE
	Orthodox: less frequent than every week	8,3	16,7	50,0	8,3	16,7	12	20,0	33,3	26,7	20,0	0,0	15	DE
	Orthodox: never	0,0	0,0	0,0	0,0	0,0	0	0,0	100,0	0,0	0,0	0,0	2	DE
	Muslim: weekly or more frequent	28,6	28,6	42,9	0,0	0,0	7	12,5	18,8	56,3	12,5	0,0	16	DE
	Muslim: less frequent than every week	11,5	26,9	38,5	23,1	0,0	26	14,3	28,6	47,6	9,5	0,0	21	DE

(Continued)

	religious practice	left	moderate left	center	moderate right	right	n	left	moderate left	center	moderate right	right	n	
	Muslim: never	0,0	37,5	62,5	0,0	0,0	8	0,0	40,0	20,0	0,0	20,0	5	DE
	Total population	**11,6**	**28,1**	**38,3**	**15,5**	**6,4**	**2707**	**12,8**	**28,5**	**38,9**	**14,9**	**4,9**	**2591**	**DE**
DK Denmark	without denomination	9,2	22,2	27,0	27,2	14,4	585	10,6	20,8	28,3	26,9	13,4	509	DK
	Roman Catholic: weekly or more frequent	0,0	0,0	0,0	100,0	0,0	1	0,0	0,0	100,0	0,0	0,0	1	DK
	Roman Catholic: less frequent than every week	0,0	50,0	0,0	16,7	33,3	6	25,0	16,7	16,7	25,0	16,7	12	DK
	Roman Catholic: never	50,0	0,0	50,0	0,0	0,0	2	50,0	0,0	0,0	0,0	50,0	4	DK
	Protestant: weekly or more frequent	0,0	8,3	41,7	33,3	16,7	24	3,2	19,4	22,6	29,0	25,8	31	DK
	Protestant: less frequent than every week	4,1	15,7	30,3	28,4	21,5	535	3,6	17,3	27,6	34,5	17,0	612	DK
	Protestant: never	3,4	15,5	34,0	29,6	17,5	206	6,9	21,8	26,4	27,0	17,8	174	DK
	Orthodox: weekly or more frequent	0,0	0,0	0,0	0,0	0,0	0	0,0	0,0	0,0	0,0	0,0	0	DK
	Orthodox: less frequent than every week	0,0	66,7	0,0	33,3	0,0	3	100,0	0,0	0,0	0,0	0,0	1	DK
	Orthodox: never	0,0	0,0	0,0	100,0	0,0	1	0,0	0,0	0,0	0,0	0,0	0	DK
	Muslim: weekly or more frequent	50,0	0,0	50,0	0,0	0,0	2	25,0	75,0	0,0	0,0	0,0	4	DK

	religious practice	left	moderate left	center	moderate right	right	n	left	moderate left	center	moderate right	right	n	
	Muslim: less frequent than every week	10,0	10,0	40,0	20,0	20,0	10	0,0	28,6	57,1	0,0	14,3	7	DK
	Muslim: never	0,0	0,0	100,0	0,0	0,0	5	0,0	0,0	0,0	33,3	66,7	3	DK
	Total population	**6,4**	**18,2**	**29,9**	**27,9**	**17,6**	**1399**	**7,1**	**19,4**	**27,8**	**29,7**	**16,0**	**1390**	**DK**
EE Estonia	without denomination	x	x	x	x	x	x	7,4	18,2	40,0	22,9	11,6	1177	EE
	Roman Catholic: weekly or more frequent	x	x	x	x	x	x	0,0	0,0	100,0	0,0	0,0	1	EE
	Roman Catholic: less frequent than every week	x	x	x	x	x	x	11,1	33,3	33,3	22,2	0,0	9	EE
	Roman Catholic: never	x	x	x	x	x	x	0,0	0,0	0,0	0,0	0,0	0	EE
	Protestant: weekly or more frequent	x	x	x	x	x	x	10,7	17,9	28,6	25,0	17,9	28	EE
	Protestant: less frequent than every week	x	x	x	x	x	X	7,1	19,4	34,7	19,4	19,4	98	EE
	Protestant: never	x	x	x	x	x	x	44,4	0,0	22,2	33,3	0,0	9	EE
	Orthodox: weekly or more frequent	x	x	x	x	x	x	13,3	33,3	40,0	13,3	0,0	15	EE
	Orthodox: less frequent than every week	x	x	x	x	x	x	17,9	24,6	41,8	9,0	6,7	134	EE
	Orthodox: never	x	x	x	x	x	x	0,0	44,4	44,4	0,0	11,1	9	EE

religious practice	left	moderate left	center	moderate right	right	n	left	moderate left	center	moderate right	right	n	
Muslim: weekly or more frequent	x	x	x	x	x	x	0,0	0,0	0,0	0,0	0,0	0	EE
Muslim: less frequent than every week	x	x	x	x	x	x	0,0	50,0	0,0	0,0	50,0	2	EE
Muslim: never	x	x	x	x	x	x	0,0	0,0	0,0	0,0	0,0	0	EE
Total pop.	x	x	x	x	x	x	**8,6**	**19,5**	**39,4**	**21,2**	**11,4**	**1500**	**EE**
ES Spain without denomination	28,7	37,7	23,1	7,8	2,8	321	29,7	36,9	23,9	5,8	3,7	377	ES
Roman Catholic: weekly or more frequent	6,3	15,3	31,7	27,6	19,0	268	7,0	17,0	30,6	24,5	21,0	220	ES
Roman Catholic: less frequent than every week	14,5	32,4	30,9	16,4	5,8	537	15,9	26,5	31,0	18,2	8,4	490	ES
Roman Catholic: never	15,9	32,9	36,2	13,0	2,0	246	16,7	30,4	33,5	10,9	8,6	257	ES
Protestant: weekly or more frequent	0,0	33,3	0,0	33,3	33,3	3	40,0	20,0	40,0	0,0	0,0	5	ES
Protestant: less frequent than every week	50,0	50,0	0,0	0,0	0,0	2	0,0	0,0	100,0	0,0	0,0	2	ES
Protestant: never	0,0	0,0	0,0	0,0	0,0	0	0,0	0,0	0,0	0,0	0,0	0	ES
Orthodox: weekly or more frequent	0,0	0,0	0,0	0,0	0,0	0	100,0	0,0	0,0	0,0	0,0	1	ES
Orthodox: less frequent than every week	0,0	0,0	0,0	0,0	0,0	0	0,0	33,3	0,0	33,3	33,3	3	ES

(Continued)

	religious practice	left	moderate left	center	moderate right	right	n	left	moderate left	center	moderate right	right	n	
	Orthodox: never	0,0	0,0	0,0	100,0	0,0	1	50,0	0,0	50,0	0,0	0,0	2	ES
	Muslim: weekly or more frequent	33,3	0,0	66,7	0,0	0,0	3	50,0	0,0	50,0	0,0	0,0	2	ES
	Muslim: less frequent than every week	0,0	0,0	0,0	0,0	0,0	0	40,0	20,0	40,0	0,0	0,0	5	ES
	Muslim: never	0,0	0,0	0,0	0,0	0,0	0	66,7	0,0	0,0	33,3	0,0	3	ES
	Total population	**16,5**	**30,2**	**30,4**	**15,8**	**7,1**	**1397**	**18,7**	**28,3**	**29,8**	**14,1**	**9,1**	**1411**	**ES**
FI Finland	without denomination	9,4	24,3	32,2	23,5	10,5	456	x	x	x	x	x	x	FI
	Roman Catholic: weekly or more frequent	0,0	0,0	0,0	0,0	0,0	0	x	x	x	x	x	x	FI
	Roman Catholic: less frequent than every week	0,0	0,0	50,0	0,0	50,0	2	x	x	x	x	x	x	FI
	Roman Catholic: never	0,0	0,0	0,0	0,0	100,0	1	x	x	x	x	x	x	FI
	Protestant: weekly or more frequent	1,4	11,6	23,2	31,9	31,9	69	x	x	x	x	x	x	FI
	Protestant: less frequent than every week	4,2	15,0	32,0	27,5	21,2	1093	x	x	x	x	x	x	FI
	religious practice	left	moderate left	center	moderate right	right	n	left	moderate left	center	moderate right	right	n	
	Protestant: never	9,7	18,9	32,3	19,8	19,4	217	x	x	x	x	x	x	FI

	religious practice	left	moderate left	center	moderate right	right	N	left	moderate left	center	moderate right	right	n	
	Orthodox: weekly or more frequent	0,0	0,0	0,0	0,0	100,0	1	x	x	x	x	x	x	FI
	Orthodox: less frequent than every week	0,0	17,6	23,5	35,3	23,5	17	x	x	x	x	x	x	FI
	Orthodox: never	0,0	0,0	50,0	50,0	0,0	2	x	x	x	x	x	x	FI
	Muslim: weekly or more frequent	0,0	0,0	0,0	0,0	0,0	0	x	x	x	x	x	x	FI
	Muslim: less frequent than every week	0,0	0,0	100,0	0,0	0,0	1	x	x	x	x	x	x	FI
	Muslim: never	0,0	0,0	100,0	0,0	0,0	1	x	x	x	x	x	x	FI
	Total population	**5,9**	**17,5**	**31,7**	**26,2**	**18,8**	**1891**	**4,9**	**16,9**	**30,7**	**25,7**	**21,8**	**1923**	**FI**
FR France	without denomination	21,8	28,2	29,8	11,3	8,9	698	22,8	26,4	33,2	11,7	5,9	823	FR
	Roman Catholic: weekly or more frequent	3,2	17,2	17,2	36,6	25,8	93	x	x	x	x	x	x	FR
	Roman Catholic: less frequent than every week	9,3	17,1	26,1	24,2	23,3	356	x	x	x	x	x	x	FR
	Roman Catholic: never	16,5	19,6	33,5	20,3	10,1	158	x	x	x	x	x	x	FR
	Protestant: weekly or more frequent	0,0	33,3	33,3	33,3	0,0	3	x	x	x	x	x	x	FR

(Continued)

	religious practice	left	moderate left	center	moderate right	right	N	left	moderate left	center	moderate right	right	n	
	Protestant: less frequent than every week	0,0	38,5	15,4	23,1	23,1	13	x	x	x	x	x	x	FR
	Protestant: never	0,0	0,0	80,0	20,0	0,0	5	x	x	x	x	x	x	FR
	Orthodox: weekly or more frequent	0,0	0,0	0,0	0,0	0,0	0	x	x	x	x	x	x	FR
	Orthodox: less frequent than every week	0,0	100,0	0,0	0,0	0,0	1	x	x	x	x	x	x	FR
	Orthodox: never	0,0	0,0	0,0	100,0	0,0	1	x	x	x	x	x	x	FR
	F Muslim: weekly or more frequent	75,0	25,0	0,0	0,0	0,0	4	x	x	x	x	x	x	FR
	Muslim: less frequent than every week	35,3	23,5	20,6	14,7	5,9	34	x	x	x	x	x	x	FR
	religious practice	left	moderate left	center	moderate right	right	N	left	moderate left	center	moderate right	right	n	
	Muslim: never	12,5	37,5	25,0	12,5	12,5	8	x	x	x	x	x	x	FR
	Total Pop.	**16,7**	**23,5**	**28,4**	**17,6**	**13,8**	**1406**	**16,8**	**22,9**	**30,4**	**17,4**	**12,4**	**1695**	**FR**
GB United Kingdom	without denomination	6,8	20,8	46,1	19,2	7,0	926	8,0	20,4	51,6	15,8	4,2	835	GB
	Roman Catholic: weekly or more frequent	5,1	21,8	42,3	17,9	12,8	78	8,2	24,7	41,1	17,8	8,2	73	GB
	Roman Catholic: less frequent than every week	0,0	19,4	50,7	26,9	3,0	67	10,5	21,1	44,7	17,1	6,6	76	GB

(Continued)

	religious practice	left	moderate left	center	moderate right	right	n	left	moderate left	center	moderate right	right	n	
	Roman Catholic: never	6,7	23,3	43,3	20,0	6,7	30	12,5	21,9	46,9	9,4	9,4	32	GB
	Protestant: weekly or more frequent	1,8	16,7	37,7	29,8	14,0	114	3,3	19,6	33,7	23,9	19,6	92	GB
	Protestant: less frequent than every week	4,4	15,2	42,5	23,8	14,1	341	4,6	15,1	47,7	22,9	9,6	218	GB
	Protestant: never	9,3	14,5	40,9	21,2	14,0	193	5,1	20,6	40,4	19,9	14,0	136	GB
	Orthodox: weekly or more frequent	0,0	0,0	0,0	0,0	0,0	0	0,0	0,0	0,0	100,0	0,0	1	GB
	Orthodox: less frequent than every week	0,0	0,0	0,0	0,0	100,0	1	0,0	0,0	100,0	0,0	0,0	2	GB
	Orthodox: never	0,0	0,0	0,0	0,0	0,0	0	0,0	0,0	66,7	0,0	33,3	3	GB
	GB Muslim: weekly or more frequent	0,0	22,2	66,7	11,1	0,0	9	6,3	12,5	62,5	18,8	0,0	16	GB
	Muslim: less frequent than every week	0,0	58,3	25,0	8,3	8,3	12	17,6	5,9	70,6	5,9	0,0	17	GB
	Muslim: never	0,0	16,7	50,0	16,7	16,7	6	0,0	14,3	57,1	14,3	14,3	7	GB
	Total population	**6,0**	**19,4**	**44,0**	**21,1**	**9,5**	**1859**	**7,2**	**19,5**	**48,3**	**17,6**	**7,4**	**1711**	**GB**
GR Greece	without denomination	21,9	21,9	28,1	14,1	14,1	64	15,3	16,9	41,2	15,8	10,7	172	GR
	Roman Catholic: weekly or more frequent	50,0	0,0	0,0	50,0	0,0	2	0,0	0,0	33,3	0,0	66,7	3	GR

(Continued)

religious practice	left	moderate left	center	moderate right	right	n	left	moderate left	center	moderate right	right	n	GR
Roman Catholic: less frequent than every week	0,0	50,0	0,0	0,0	50,0	2	0,0	33,3	41,7	16,7	8,3	12	GR
Roman Catholic: never	0,0	0,0	33,3	33,3	33,3	3	0,0	0,0	0,0	0,0	0,0	0	GR
Protestant: weekly or more frequent	0,0	50,0	0,0	0,0	50,0	2	100,0	0,0	0,0	0,0	0,0	1	GR
religious practice	left	moderate left	center	moderate right	right	n	left	moderate left	center	moderate right	right	n	
Protestant: less frequent than every week	0,0	20,0	40,0	40,0	0,0	5	0,0	50,0	0,0	50,0	0,0	2	GR
Protestant: never	0,0	0,0	0,0	0,0	0,0	0	0,0	0,0	0,0	0,0	0,0	0	GR
Orthodox: weekly or more frequent	3,1	9,8	37,9	14,1	35,0	488	4,2	9,9	30,9	20,8	34,2	456	GR
Orthodox: less frequent than every week	6,1	18,9	40,0	13,9	21,1	1320	7,8	14,8	36,9	19,4	21,1	1236	GR
Orthodox: never	14,0	32,0	24,0	8,0	22,0	50	22,2	25,0	36,1	0,0	16,7	36	GR
Muslim: weekly or more frequent	0,0	12,5	37,5	12,5	37,5	8	0,0	0,0	66,7	33,3	0,0	9	GR
Muslim: less frequent than every week	5,3	15,8	63,2	5,3	10,5	19	0,0	0,0	20,0	40,0	40,0	5	GR
Muslim: never	14,3	0,0	85,7	0,0	0,0	7	0,0	28,6	57,1	0,0	14,3	7	GR
Total population	**6,1**	**17,0**	**39,1**	**13,7**	**24,1**	**1983**	**7,8**	**14,1**	**36,0**	**19,1**	**23,0**	**1947**	**GR**

	religious practice	left	moderate left	center	moderate right	right	n	left	moderate left	center	moderate right	right	n	HU
HU Hungary	without denomination	17,5	22,0	36,8	11,5	12,1	513	15,5	25,1	36,0	15,3	8,1	458	HU
	Roman Catholic: weekly or more frequent	9,4	18,1	22,8	22,0	27,6	127	x	x	x	x	x	x	HU
	Roman Catholic: less frequent than every week	12,3	22,8	30,1	17,8	17,0	399	x	x	x	x	x	x	HU
	Roman Catholic: never	20,2	25,3	28,3	13,1	13,1	99	x	x	x	x	x	x	HU
	Protestant: weekly or more frequent	0,0	21,7	17,4	34,8	26,1	23	x	x	x	x	x	x	HU
	Protestant: less frequent than every week	10,6	16,3	39,4	16,9	16,9	160	x	x	x	x	x	x	HU
	Protestant: never	25,5	25,5	15,7	15,7	17,6	51	x	x	x	x	x	x	HU
	Orthodox: weekly or more frequent	0,0	0,0	0,0	0,0	0,0	0	x	x	x	x	x	x	HU
	Orthodox: less frequent than every week	0,0	0,0	0,0	0,0	100,0	1	x	x	x	x	x	x	HU
	Orthodox: never	100,0	0,0	0,0	0,0	0,0	1	X	x	x	x	x	x	HU
	Muslim: weekly or more frequent	0,0	0,0	0,0	0,0	0,0	0	x	x	x	x	x	x	HU
	Muslim: less frequent than every week	0,0	0,0	0,0	0,0	0,0	0	x	x	x	x	x	x	HU

(Continued)

	religious practice	left	moderate left	center	moderate right	right	N	left	moderate left	center	moderate right	right	n	
	Muslim: never	0,0	0,0	0,0	0,0	0,0	0	x	x	x	x	x	x	HU
	Total population	**14,8**	**21,5**	**32,4**	**15,4**	**16,0**	**139 8**	**12,9**	**18,8**	**35,8**	**18,2**	**14,2**	**1229**	**HU**
IE Ireland	without denomination	9,9	25,1	42,0	14,5	8,5	283	9,7	28,2	42,0	13,0	7,1	238	IE
	Roman Catholic: weekly or more frequent	3,6	10,8	39,0	27,6	18,9	830	2,3	12,1	50,7	21,7	13,2	1064	IE
	Roman Catholic: less frequent than every week	5,6	20,8	41,8	20,1	11,6	447	5,7	24,2	42,4	21,0	6,7	495	IE
	Roman Catholic: never	12,8	17,0	40,4	17,0	12,8	47	4,8	19,0	38,1	23,8	14,3	42	IE
	Protestant: weekly or more frequent	3,6	14,3	39,3	32,1	10,7	28	0,0	15,4	42,3	23,1	19,2	26	IE
	Protestant: less frequent than every week	8,0	16,0	44,0	16,0	16,0	25	3,2	9,7	61,3	19,4	6,5	31	IE
	Protestant: never	100,0	0,0	0,0	0,0	0,0	1	0,0	100,0	0,0	0,0	0,0	1	IE
	Orthodox: weekly or more frequent	0,0	0,0	0,0	0,0	0,0	0	0,0	0,0	0,0	0,0	0,0	0	IE
	Orthodox: less frequent than every week	0,0	0,0	0,0	0,0	0,0	0	0,0	0,0	0,0	0,0	0,0	0	IE
	Orthodox: never	0,0	0,0	0,0	0,0	0,0	0	0,0	0,0	0,0	0,0	0,0	0	IE
	Muslim: weekly or more frequent	0,0	0,0	0,0	0,0	100,0	1	0,0	0,0	0,0	0,0	0,0	0	IE

(Continued)

religious practice	left	moderate left	center	moderate right	right	N	left	moderate left	center	moderate right	right	n	
Muslim: less frequent than every week	0,0	0,0	0,0	100,0	0,0	1	0,0	0,0	0,0	0,0	0,0	0	IE
Muslim: never	0,0	0,0	0,0	0,0	0,0	0	0,0	0,0	0,0	0,0	0,0	0	IE
Total population	**5,7**	**16,1**	**40,6**	**22,9**	**14,7**	**1695**	**4,2**	**17,6**	**47,1**	**20,4**	**10,7**	**1915**	**IE**
IS Iceland — without denomination	x	x	x	x	x	x	12,0	24,3	27,9	21,7	14,1	276	IS
Roman Catholic: weekly or more frequent	x	x	x	x	x	x	0,0	0,0	0,0	0,0	0,0	0	IS
Roman Catholic: less frequent than every week	x	x	x	x	x	x	0,0	0,0	0,0	0,0	0,0	0	IS
Roman Catholic: never	x	x	x	x	x	x	0,0	0,0	0,0	0,0	0,0	0	IS
religious practice	left	moderate left	center	moderate right	right	n	left	moderate left	center	moderate right	right	n	
Protestant: weekly or more frequent	x	x	x	x	x	x	0,0	25,0	33,3	41,7	0,0	12	IS
Protestant: less frequent than every week	x	x	x	x	x	x	5,5	25,6	32,3	25,6	11,0	164	IS
Protestant: never	x	x	x	x	x	x	12,5	23,2	28,6	26,8	8,9	56	IS
Orthodox: weekly or more frequent	x	x	x	x	x	x	0,0	0,0	0,0	0,0	0,0	0	IS
Orthodox: less frequent than every week	x	x	x	x	x	x	0,0	0,0	0,0	0,0	0,0	0	IS

(Continued)

	religious practice	left	moderate left	center	moderate right	right	N	left	moderate left	center	moderate right	right	n	
	Orthodox: never	x	x	x	x	x	x	0,0	0,0	0,0	0,0	0,0	0	IS
	Muslim: weekly or more frequent	x	x	x	x	x	x	0,0	0,0	0,0	0,0	0,0	0	IS
	Muslim: less frequent than every week	x	x	x	x	x	x	0,0	0,0	0,0	0,0	0,0	0	IS
	Muslim: never	x	x	x	x	x	x	0,0	0,0	0,0	0,0	0,0	0	IS
	Total population	**x**	**x**	**x**	**x**	**x**	**x**	**9,8**	**24,2**	**29,1**	**24,0**	**12,9**	**533**	**IS**
IL Israel	without denomination	19,7	20,0	24,4	13,4	22,5	574	x	x	x	x	x	x	IL
	Roman Catholic: weekly or more frequent	60,0	6,7	26,7	6,7	0,0	15	x	x	x	x	x	x	IL
	Roman Catholic: less frequent than every week	69,5	11,9	18,6	0,0	0,0	59	x	x	x	x	x	x	IL
	Roman Catholic: never	58,3	0,0	25,0	16,7	0,0	12	x	x	x	x	x	x	IL
	Protestant: weekly or more frequent	0,0	0,0	0,0	0,0	0,0	0	x	x	x	x	x	x	IL
	Protestant: less frequent than every week	0,0	0,0	0,0	0,0	0,0	0	x	x	x	x	x	x	IL
	Protestant: never	0,0	0,0	0,0	0,0	0,0	0	x	x	x	x	x	x	IL
	Orthodox: weekly or more frequent	0,0	0,0	0,0	0,0	0,0	0	x	x	x	x	x	x	IL

religious practice	left	moderate left	center	moderate right	right	N	left	moderate left	center	moderate right	right	n	
Orthodox: less frequent than every week	0,0	0,0	0,0	0,0	0,0	0	x	x	x	x	x	x	IL
Orthodox: never	0,0	0,0	0,0	0,0	0,0	0	x	x	x	x	x	x	IL
religious practice	left	moderate left	center	moderate right	right	N	left	moderate left	center	moderate right	right	n	
Muslim: weekly or more frequent	64,3	15,3	13,3	2,0	5,1	98	x	x	x	x	x	x	IL
Muslim: less frequent than every week	67,2	13,4	13,9	3,5	2,0	201	x	x	x	x	x	x	IL
Muslim: never	66,7	8,3	16,7	0,0	8,3	24	x	x	x	x	x	x	IL
Total population	**21,5**	**14,4**	**20,5**	**13,8**	**29,8**	**2301**	**x**	**x**	**x**	**x**	**x**	**x**	**IL**
without denomination	24,8	30,2	18,9	15,3	10,8	222	x	x	x	x	x	x	IT
Roman Catholic: weekly or more frequent	11,6	24,0	28,3	20,9	15,1	258	x	x	x	x	x	x	IT
Roman Catholic: less frequent than every week	13,0	22,1	28,3	24,9	11,7	385	x	x	x	x	x	x	IT
Roman Catholic: never	22,2	33,3	20,4	13,0	11,1	54	x	x	x	x	x	x	IT
Protestant: weekly or more frequent	25,0	25,0	50,0	0,0	0,0	4	x	x	x	x	x	x	IT
Protestant: less frequent than every week	0,0	0,0	66,7	33,3	0,0	3	x	x	x	x	x	x	IT

IT Italy

	religious practice	left	moderate left	center	moderate right	right	N	left	moderate left	center	moderate right	right	n	
	Protestant: never	0,0	100,0	0,0	0,0	0,0	1	x	x	x	x	x	x	IT
	Orthodox: weekly or more frequent	0,0	0,0	0,0	0,0	0,0	0	x	x	x	x	x	x	IT
	Orthodox: less frequent than every week	0,0	0,0	0,0	0,0	0,0	0	x	x	x	x	x	x	IT
	Orthodox: never	0,0	0,0	0,0	0,0	0,0	0	x	x	x	x	x	x	IT
	Muslim: weekly or more frequent	0,0	0,0	0,0	0,0	0,0	0	x	x	x	x	x	x	IT
	Muslim: less frequent than every week	0,0	0,0	0,0	0,0	0,0	0	x	x	x	x	x	x	IT
	Muslim: never	0,0	100,0	0,0	0,0	0,0	1	x	x	x	x	x	x	IT
	Total population	**15,8**	**25,3**	**25,8**	**20,6**	**12,4**	**935**	**x**	**x**	**x**	**x**	**x**	**x**	**IT**
LU Luxembourg	without denomination	19,1	22,3	40,1	13,2	5,3	319	11,7	23,5	42,1	16,1	6,6	409	LU
	Roman Catholic: weekly or more frequent	6,8	3,0	45,9	21,1	23,3	133	3,1	6,9	39,7	19,1	31,3	131	LU
	Roman Catholic: less frequent than every week	9,3	14,9	37,2	22,6	16,1	323	7,8	13,6	44,1	22,1	12,3	447	LU

(Continued)

	religious practice	left	moderate left	center	moderate right	right	n	left	moderate left	center	moderate right	right	n	
	Roman Catholic: never	18,4	22,1	39,3	11,7	8,6	163	6,3	22,8	48,8	8,7	13,4	127	LU
	Protestant: weekly or more frequent	0,0	0,0	0,0	0,0	0,0	0	0,0	0,0	0,0	0,0	0,0	0	LU
	Protestant: less frequent than every week	0,0	14,3	28,6	57,1	0,0	7	0,0	37,5	50,0	12,5	0,0	8	LU
	Protestant: never	20,0	0,0	0,0	60,0	20,0	5	0,0	0,0	50,0	0,0	50,0	2	LU
	Orthodox: weekly or more frequent	0,0	0,0	50,0	50,0	0,0	2	0,0	0,0	0,0	0,0	100,0	1	LU
	Orthodox: less frequent than every week	0,0	50,0	50,0	0,0	0,0	2	0,0	0,0	0,0	0,0	100,0	1	LU
	Orthodox: never	0,0	50,0	50,0	0,0	0,0	2	0,0	0,0	50,0	50,0	0,0	2	LU
	Muslim: weekly or more frequent	0,0	0,0	100,0	0,0	0,0	1	0,0	0,0	0,0	0,0	0,0	0	LU
	Muslim: less frequent than every week	33,3	0,0	66,7	0,0	0,0	3	0,0	33,3	66,7	0,0	0,0	3	LU
	Muslim: never	0,0	41,7	50,0	0,0	8,3	12	0,0	0,0	25,0	0,0	75,0	4	LU
	Total population	**12,9**	**16,4**	**41,4**	**17,2**	**12,2**	**1198**	**8,9**	**17,3**	**43,5**	**17,0**	**13,4**	**131**	**LU**
NL Netherlands	without denomination	11,2	24,7	27,9	25,7	10,6	1277	13,4	28,1	26,3	22,9	9,4	95	NL
	Roman Catholic: weekly or more frequent	2,7	9,6	37,0	35,6	15,1	73	1,5	15,2	33,3	28,8	21,2	66	NL

(Continued)

religious practice	left	moderate left	center	moderate right	right	n	left	moderate left	center	moderate right	right	n	NL
Roman Catholic: less frequent than every week	5,8	19,9	29,2	30,8	14,4	312	6,8	16,7	28,8	37,9	9,8	264	NL
Roman Catholic: never	9,4	20,3	31,3	29,7	9,4	64	7,7	19,2	35,9	23,1	14,1	78	NL
Protestant: weekly or more frequent	2,6	13,0	14,3	40,3	29,9	154	2,3	8,4	24,4	32,8	32,1	131	NL
Protestant: less frequent than every week	6,4	15,4	26,9	33,3	17,9	156	4,0	18,3	24,6	42,9	10,3	126	NL
Protestant: never	8,8	14,0	19,3	33,3	24,6	57	1,6	16,4	27,9	39,3	14,8	61	NL
Orthodox: weekly or more frequent	0,0	0,0	0,0	0,0	0,0	0.	0,0	0,0	0,0	0,0	0,0	0	NL
religious practice	Left	moderate left	center	moderate right	right	N	left	moderate left	center	moderate right	right	right	NL
Orthodox: less frequent than every week	0,0	0,0	50,0	50,0	0,0	2	0,0	0,0	100,0	0,0	0,0	2	NL
Orthodox: never	0,0	100,0	0,0	0,0	0,0	1	0,0	100,0	0,0	0,0	0,0	1	NL
Muslim: weekly or more frequent	11,1	11,1	22,2	33,3	22,2	9	25,0	75,0	0,0	0,0	0,0	4	NL
Muslim: less frequent than every week	16,7	22,2	27,8	27,8	5,6	18	20,0	30,0	20,0	20,0	10,0	10	NL
Muslim: never	22,2	33,3	44,4	0,0	0,0	9	14,3	14,3	57,1	14,3	0,0	7	NL
Total population	**9,1**	**21,5**	**27,0**	**28,8**	**13,6**	**2254**	**9,7**	**23,0**	**27,2**	**28,1**	**12,0**	**1778**	**NL**

(Continued)

	religious practice	left	moderate left	center	moderate right	right	n	left	moderate left	center	moderate right	right	n	NO
NO Norway	without denomination	8,2	27,4	24,0	25,6	14,8	974	10,1	31,5	21,4	23,3	13,7	854	NO
	Roman Catholic: weekly or more frequent	0,0	0,0	0,0	0,0	100,0	1	0,0	0,0	50,0	25,0	25,0	4	NO
	Roman Catholic: less frequent than every week	0,0	28,6	14,3	28,6	28,6	7	9,1	36,4	18,2	9,1	27,3	11	NO
	Roman Catholic: never	0,0	40,0	20,0	40,0	0,0	5	0,0	100,0	0,0	0,0	0,0	2	NO
	Protestant: weekly or more frequent	1,8	29,1	18,2	30,9	20,0	55	4,0	18,0	36,0	30,0	12,0	50	NO
	Protestant: less frequent than every week	4,6	25,1	26,9	28,3	15,2	658	8,2	30,5	26,6	22,3	12,5	53	NO
	Protestant: never	6,3	18,8	26,2	33,0	15,7	191	7,8	31,1	24,0	24,0	13,2	167	NO
	Orthodox: weekly or more frequent	0,0	0,0	0,0	0,0	0,0	0	0,0	100,0	0,0	0,0	0,0	1	NO
	Orthodox: less frequent than every week	0,0	25,0	50,0	0,0	25,0	4	0,0	0,0	20,0	80,0	0,0	5	NO
	Orthodox: never	0,0	0,0	0,0	0,0	0,0	0	0,0	0,0	100,0	0,0	0,0	1	NO
	Muslim: weekly or more frequent	0,0	50,0	50,0	0,0	0,0	2	0,0	50,0	16,7	33,3	0,0	6	NO
	Muslim: less frequent than every week	22,2	0,0	33,3	22,2	22,2	9	0,0	20,0	60,0	10,0	10,0	10	NO

(Continued)

	religious practice	left	moderate left	center	moderate right	right	n	left	moderate left	center	moderate right	right	n	
	Muslim: never	28,6	14,3	42,9	0,0	14,3	7	20,0	20,0	0,0	40,0	20,0	5	NO
	Total population	**6,5**	**25,7**	**25,3**	**27,3**	**15,1**	**1987**	**8,9**	**30,3**	**24,0**	**23,5**	**13,2**	**1722**	**NO**
PL Poland	without denomination	23,6	25,7	31,9	7,6	11,1	144	13,5	23,4	38,7	7,2	17,1	111	PL
	religious practice	Left	moderate left	center	moderate right	right	N	left	moderate left	center	moderate right	right	n	
	Roman Catholic: weekly or more frequent	10,0	15,2	35,7	18,2	20,8	946	7,4	12,5	36,2	23,3	20,7	774	PL
	Roman Catholic: less frequent than every week	16,6	19,1	37,3	13,0	14,0	614	12,3	15,8	39,5	17,3	15,1	456	PL
	Roman Catholic: never	20,0	15,0	45,0	10,0	10,0	20	25,0	6,3	25,0	25,0	18,8	16	PL
	Protestant: weekly or more frequent	100,0	0,0	0,0	0,0	0,0	1	0,0	0,0	0,0	100,0	0,0	1	PL
	Protestant: less frequent than every week	0,0	0,0	100,0	0,0	0,0	1	100,0	0,0	0,0	0,0	0,0	1	PL
	Protestant: never	0,0	0,0	0,0	0,0	0,0	0	0,0	0,0	100,0	0,0	0,0	1	PL
	Orthodox: weekly or more frequent	66,7	0,0	33,3	0,0	0,0	3	0,0	0,0	0,0	0,0	0,0	0	PL
	Orthodox: less frequent than every week	33,3	22,2	44,4	0,0	0,0	9	12,5	12,5	50,0	12,5	12,5	8	PL
	Orthodox: never	0,0	0,0	0,0	0,0	0,0	0	0,0	0,0	0,0	0,0	0,0	0	PL

(Continued)

	religious practice	left	moderate left	center	moderate right	right	n	left	moderate left	center	moderate right	right	n	
	Muslim: weekly or more frequent	0,0	0,0	0,0	0,0	0,0	0	0,0	0,0	0,0	0,0	0,0	0	PL
	Muslim: less frequent than every week	0,0	0,0	0,0	0,0	0,0	0	0,0	0,0	0,0	0,0	100,0	1	PL
	Muslim: never	0,0	0,0	0,0	0,0	0,0	0	0,0	0,0	0,0	0,0	0,0	0	PL
	Total population	**13,9**	**17,5**	**36,1**	**15,1**	**17,4**	**1757**	**9,7**	**14,5**	**37,5**	**19,8**	**18,5**	**137**	**PL**
PT Portugal	without denomination	16,6	33,2	28,3	14,6	7,3	205	17,1	36,7	28,1	12,4	5,7	210	PT
	Roman Catholic: weekly or more frequent	7,9	21,3	27,3	25,1	18,4	315	9,8	23,2	25,4	23,7	17,9	358	PT
	Roman Catholic: less frequent than every week	12,7	26,9	27,9	20,7	11,9	513	10,6	28,6	25,3	18,5	17,0	615	PT
	Roman Catholic: never	15,5	25,6	28,7	20,9	9,3	129	13,5	31,2	27,7	19,1	8,5	141	PT
	Protestant: weekly or more frequent	0,0	22,2	11,1	55,6	11,1	9	0,0	40,0	20,0	20,0	20,0	5	PT
	Protestant: less frequent than every week	0,0	0,0	0,0	0,0	0,0	0	0,0	0,0	0,0	0,0	100,0	1	PT
	Protestant: never	50,0	50,0	0,0	0,0	0,0	2	0,0	0,0	0,0	0,0	0,0	0	PT
	religious practice	left	moderate left	center	moderate right	right	n	left	moderate left	center	moderate right	right	n	
	Orthodox: weekly or more frequent	0,0	0,0	0,0	0,0	0,0	0	0,0	0,0	0,0	0,0	0,0	0	PT

(Continued)

religious practice	left	moderate left	center	moderate right	right	n	left	moderate left	center	moderate right	right	n	
Orthodox: less frequent than every week	0,0	0,0	0,0	0,0	0,0	0	0,0	0,0	0,0	0,0	0,0	0	PT
Orthodox: never	100,0	0,0	0,0	0,0	0,0	1	0,0	0,0	0,0	0,0	0,0	0	PT
Muslim: weekly or more frequent	0,0	0,0	0,0	0,0	0,0	0	0,0	0,0	100,0	0,0	0,0	1	PT
Muslim: less frequent than every week	0,0	0,0	0,0	0,0	0,0	0	0,0	0,0	0,0	0,0	0,0	0	PT
Muslim: never	0,0	0,0	0,0	0,0	0,0	0	0,0	0,0	0,0	0,0	0,0	0	PT
Total population	**12,6**	**26,2**	**27,7**	**21,0**	**12,4**	**1204**	**11,8**	**28,7**	**26,2**	**18,9**	**14,5**	**1370**	**PT**
SE Sweden — without denomination	18,2	24,9	21,6	20,6	14,7	1327	12,9	22,7	27,1	21,6	15,7	1264	SE
Roman Catholic: weekly or more frequent	0,0	0,0	0,0	0,0	0,0	0	0,0	0,0	66,7	33,3	0,0	3	SE
Roman Catholic: less frequent than every week	20,0	33,3	20,0	20,0	6,7	15	7,1	21,4	14,3	21,4	35,7	14	SE
Roman Catholic: never	33,3	0,0	66,7	0,0	0,0	3	0,0	0,0	100,0	0,0	0,0	2	SE
Protestant: weekly or more frequent	3,4	18,6	25,4	32,2	20,3	59	4,9	19,5	31,7	24,4	19,5	41	SE
Protestant: less frequent than every week	13,0	21,2	23,3	21,8	20,6	330	7,7	16,5	29,0	28,2	18,6	376	SE
Protestant: never	13,1	27,4	25,0	16,7	17,9	84	10,6	22,3	24,5	21,3	21,3	94	SE

	religious practice	left	moderate left	center	moderate right	right	n	left	moderate left	center	moderate right	right	n	
	Orthodox: weekly or more frequent	0,0	0,0	0,0	0,0	0,0	0	0,0	100,0	0,0	0,0	0,0	2	SE
	Orthodox: less frequent than every week	50,0	25,0	0,0	12,5	12,5	8	20,0	0,0	20,0	40,0	20,0	5	SE
	Orthodox: never	0,0	0,0	100,0	0,0	0,0	1	0,0	0,0	0,0	0,0	0,0	0	SE
	Muslim: weekly or more frequent	0,0	50,0	50,0	0,0	0,0	2	0,0	0,0	0,0	0,0	0,0	0	SE
	Muslim: less frequent than every week	29,4	17,6	23,5	29,4	0,0	17	0,0	33,3	50,0	0,0	16,7	6	SE
	Muslim: never	33,3	0,0	16,7	33,3	16,7	6	16,7	50,0	16,7	16,7	0,0	6	SE
	Total population	**16,8**	**24,0**	**22,2**	**21,0**	**16,0**	**1891**	**11,6**	**21,2**	**27,5**	**23,0**	**16,7**	**1855**	**SE**
SI Slovenia	without denomination	22,0	22,5	43,5	6,4	5,6	605	20,4	17,8	46,1	8,3	7,4	230	SI
	Roman Catholic: weekly or more frequent	3,2	8,5	37,0	28,0	23,3	189	2,2	8,9	33,3	22,2	33,3	90	SI
	Roman Catholic: weekly or more frequent	7,0	12,7	59,0	13,0	8,3	315	11,4	15,2	42,6	14,5	16,3	280	SI
	Roman Catholic: less frequent than every week	17,6	14,7	41,2	14,7	11,8	34	26,9	20,0	36,9	7,7	8,5	151	SI
	Roman Catholic: never Protestant: weekly or more frequent	0,0	0,0	0,0	0,0	100,0	1	50,0	0,0	50,0	0,0	0,0	2	SI

(Continued)

	religious practice	left	moderate left	center	moderate right	right	N	left	moderate left	center	moderate right	right	n	
	Protestant: less frequent than every week	0,0	25,0	50,0	0,0	25,0	4	0,0	42,9	57,1	0,0	0,0	7	SI
	Protestant: never	0,0	0,0	0,0	0,0	0,0	0	0,0	0,0	0,0	0,0	0,0	0	SI
	Orthodox: weekly or more frequent	0,0	0,0	0,0	100,0	0,0	1	0,0	0,0	0,0	50,0	50,0	2	SI
	Orthodox: less frequent than every week	27,3	18,2	45,5	9,1	0,0	11	0,0	66,7	16,7	16,7	0,0	6	SI
	Orthodox: never	0,0	0,0	50,0	0,0	50,0	2	20,0	20,0	20,0	40,0	0,0	5	SI
	Muslim: weekly or more frequent	100,0	0,0	0,0	0,0	0,0	1	0,0	0,0	100,0	0,0	0,0	1	SI
	Muslim: less frequent than every week	0,0	0,0	100,0	0,0	0,0	6	0,0	0,0	100,0	0,0	0,0	4	SI
	Muslim: never	40,0	0,0	60,0	0,0	0,0	5	33,3	33,3	33,3	0,0	0,0	3	SI
	Total population	**14,6**	**17,2**	**46,8**	**12,1**	**9,4**	**1195**	**13,3**	**15,5**	**42,7**	**13,6**	**14,8**	**1034**	**SI**
SK Slovakia	without denomination	x	x	x	x	x	x	16,7	21,9	31,7	13,1	16,7	306	SK
	Roman Catholic: weekly or more frequent	x	x	x	x	x	x	15,6	17,7	33,2	15,3	18,3	334	SK
	Roman Catholic: less frequent than every week	x	x	x	x	x	x	14,6	23,4	35,4	16,1	10,5	342	SK
	Roman Catholic: never	x	x	x	x	x	x	32,6	17,4	26,1	13,0	10,9	46	SK

(Continued)

	religious practice	left	moderate left	center	moderate right	right	n	left	moderate left	center	moderate right	right	n	
	Protestant: weekly or more frequent	x	x	x	x	x	x	15,0	35,0	30,0	10,0	10,0	20	SK
	Protestant: less frequent than every week	x	x	x	x	x	x	16,1	23,2	35,7	16,1	8,9	56	SK
	Protestant: never	x	x	x	x	x	x	27,3	18,2	36,4	9,1	9,1	11	SK
	Orthodox: weekly or more frequent	x	x	x	x	x	x	0,0	40,0	60,0	0,0	0,0	5	SK
	Orthodox: less frequent than every week	x	x	x	x	x	x	14,3	28,6	57,1	0,0	0,0	7	SK
	Orthodox: never	x	x	x	x	x	x	0,0	50,0	0,0	0,0	50,0	2	SK
	Muslim: weekly or more frequent	x	x	x	x	x	x	0,0	100,0	0,0	0,0	0,0	1	SK
	Muslim: less frequent than every week	x	x	x	x	x	x	0,0	0,0	0,0	100,0	0,0	1	SK
	Muslim: never	x	x	x	x	x	x	0,0	0,0	0,0	0,0	0,0	0	SK
	Total population	x	x	x	x	x	x	**15,5**	**20,9**	**33,7**	**15,1**	**14,7**	**1225**	**SK**
UA Ukraine	without denomination	x	x	x	x	x	x	14,6	14,3	40,6	16,4	14,0	34	UA
	Roman Catholic: weekly or more frequent	x	x	x	x	x	x	0,0	5,5	16,4	12,7	65,5	55	UA

(Continued)

religious practice	left	moderate left	center	moderate right	right	N	left	moderate left	center	moderate right	right	n	
Roman Catholic: less frequent than every week	x	x	x	x	x	X	0,0	12,0	16,9	20,5	50,6	83	UA
Roman Catholic: never	x	x	x	x	x	X	0,0	0,0	0,0	20,0	80,0	5	UA
Protestant: weekly or more frequent	x	x	x	x	x	x	5,9	5,9	41,2	23,5	23,5	17	UA
Protestant: less frequent than every week	x	x	x	x	x	x	0,0	50,0	0,0	0,0	50,0	2	UA
Protestant: never	x	x	x	x	x	x	0,0	0,0	0,0	0,0	0,0	0	UA
Orthodox: weekly or more frequent	x	x	x	x	x	x	10,7	6,0	47,6	9,5	26,2	84	UA
Orthodox: less frequent than every week	x	x	x	x	x	x	13,2	11,6	39,4	14,1	21,6	619	UA
Orthodox: never	x	x	x	x	x	x	29,6	11,1	37,0	9,3	13,0	54	UA
Muslim: weekly or more frequent	x	x	x	x	x	x	0,0	0,0	0,0	0,0	0,0	0	UA
Muslim: less frequent than every week	x	x	x	x	x	x	0,0	50,0	0,0	0,0	50,0	2	UA
Muslim: never	x	x	x	x	x	x	100,0	0,0	0,0	0,0	0,0	1	UA
Total pop	**X**	**x**	**x**	**x**	**x**	**x**	**12,2**	**11,8**	**37,5**	**14,8**	**23,8**	**1327**	**UA**

THE DYNAMICS OF POLITICAL ATTITUDES IN EUROPE AND ISRAEL, 2002 – 2004

The size of the political center – all denominations

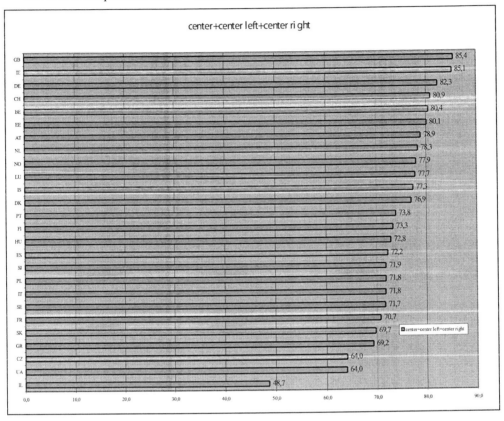

General population, political dynamics – dyn extreme left.

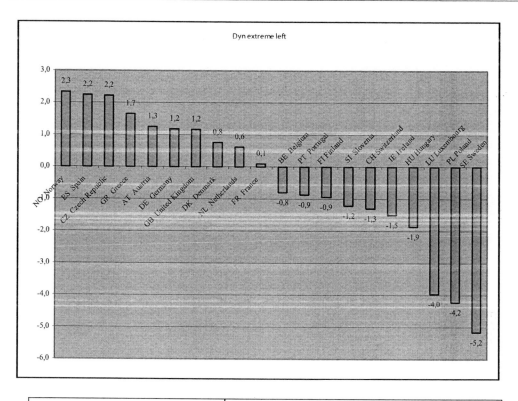

	Dyn extreme left
NO Norway	2,3
ES Spain	2,2
CZ Czech Republic	2,2
GR Greece	1,7
AT Austria	*1,3*
DE Germany	1,2
GB United Kingdom	1,2
DK Denmark	0,8
NL Netherlands	0,6
FR France	0,1
BE Belgium	-0,8
PT Portugal	-0,9
FI Finland	-0,9
SI Slovenia	-1,2
CH Switzerland	-1,3
IE Ireland	-1,5
HU Hungary	-1,9
LU Luxembourg	-4,0
PL Poland	-4,2
SE Sweden	-5,2

General population, political dynamics – dyn center

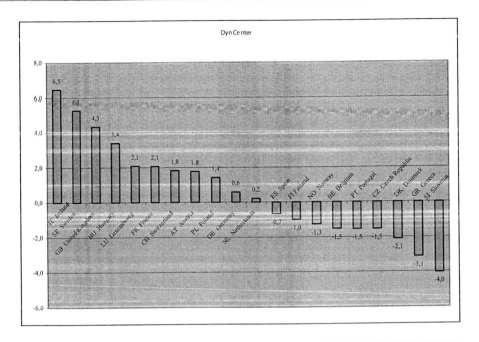

	Dyn Center
IE Ireland	6,5
SE Sweden	5,3
GB United Kingdom	4,3
HU Hungary	3,4
LU Luxembourg	2,1
FR France	2,1
CH Switzerland	1,8
AT Austria	1,8
PL Poland	1,4
DE Germany	0,6
NL Netherlands	0,2
ES Spain	-0,7
FI Finland	-1,0
NO Norway	-1,3
BE Belgium	-1,5
PT Portugal	-1,5
CZ Czech Republic	-1,5
DK Denmark	-2,1
GR Greece	-3,1
SI Slovenia	-4,0

General population, political dynamics – dyn extreme right.

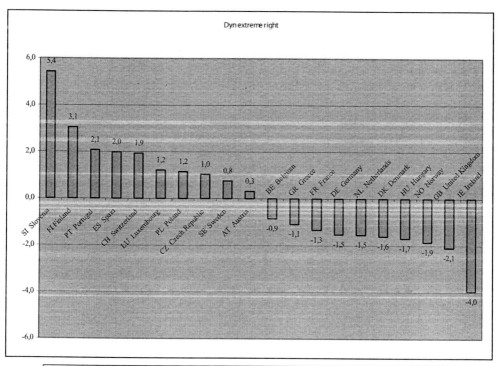

	Dyn extreme right
SI Slovenia	5,4
FI Finland	3,1
PT Portugal	2,1
ES Spain	2,0
CH Switzerland	1,9
LU Luxembourg	1,2
PL Poland	1,2
CZ Czech Republic	1,0
SE Sweden	0,8
AT Austria	0,3
BE Belgium	-0,9
GR Greece	-1,1
FR France	-1,3
DE Germany	-1,5
NL Netherlands	-1,5
DK Denmark	-1,6
HU Hungary	-1,7
NO Norway	-1,9
GB United Kingdom	-2,1
IE Ireland	-4,0

6. THE GAPS IN TRUST IN PARLIAMENT, LEGAL SYSTEM, POLICE, DEMOCRACY AND THE GAPS IN REAL INCOMES AND POVERTY, MUSLIM POPULATION AND NON-MUSLIM POPULATION. ESS DATA 2002 AND 2004

	low trust in Parliament 2002	low trust in Parliament 2004		low trust in parliament 2002	low trust in Parliament 2004		low trust in Parliament 2002	low trust in Parliament 2004	DYN relative discrimination
Austria Muslims	28,6	37	Austria non-Muslims	23	26,7	Austria implied discrimination	5,6	10,3	4,7
Belgium Muslims	16,1	21,4	Belgium non-Muslims	20,7	24,8	Belgium implied discrimination	-4,6	-3,4	1,2
Denmark Muslims	26,3	31,4	Denmark non-Muslims	10	9,4	Denmark implied discrimination	16,3	22	5,7
France Muslims	31,4		France non-Muslims	24		France implied discrimination	7,4		
Germany Muslims	37,7	34,5	Germany non-Muslims	29,4	34,1	Germany implied discrimination	8,3	0,4	-7,9
Greece Muslims	8,3	14,6	Greece non-Muslims	31,9	28,8	Greece implied discrimination	-23,6	-14,2	9,4
Israel Muslims	41,7		Israel non-Muslims	32,3		Israel implied discrimination	9,4		
Luxembourg Muslims	35,4	0	Luxembourg non-Muslims	12,6	12,1	Luxembourg implied discrimination	22,8	-12,1	-34,9
Netherlands Muslims	13,1	48,1	Netherlands non-Muslims	16,1	23	Netherlands implied discrimination	-3	25,1	28,1
Norway Muslims	15,8	9,6	Norway non-Muslims	13,6	17,4	Norway implied discrimination	2,2	-7,8	-10
Slovenia Muslims	77,8	50	Slovenia non-Muslims	43,4	40,3	Slovenia implied discrimination	34,4	9,7	-24,7

(Continued)

	low trust in Parliament 2002	low trust in Parliament 2004		low trust in parliament 2002	low trust in Parliament 2004		low trust in Parliament 2002	low trust in Parliament 2004	DYN relative discrimination
Spain Muslims	50	31,7	Spain non-Muslims	25,3	19,1	Spain implied discrimination	24,7	12,6	-12,1
Sweden Muslims	4,2	16,7	Sweden non-Muslims	11,9	20,7	Sweden implied discrimination	-7,7	-4	3,7
Switzerland Muslims	10	16	Switzerland non-Muslims	9,9	13,6	Switzerland implied discrimination	0,1	2,4	2,3
UK Muslims	14,4	17,8	UK non-Muslims	27,7	35,7	UK implied discrimination	-13,3	-17,9	-4,6
Austria Muslims	17,1	35,6	Austria non-Muslims	13,3	14	Austria implied discrimination	3,8	21,6	17,8
Belgium Muslims	11,1	22,3	Belgium non-Muslims	33,6	26	Belgium implied discrimination	-22,5	-3,7	18,8
Denmark Muslims	22,2	17,7	Denmark non-Muslims	7,5	6	Denmark implied discrimination	14,7	11,7	-3
France Muslims	28,9		France non-Muslims	25		France implied discrimination	3,9		
Germany Muslims	26,4	22,3	Germany non-Muslims	15,5	18,3	Germany implied discrimination	10,9	4	-6,9
Greece Muslims	4,5	14,3	Greece non-Muslims	17,1	23,6	Greece implied discrimination	-12,6	-9,3	3,3
Israel Muslims	16,4		Israel non-Muslims	15		Israel implied discrimination	1,4		
Luxembourg Muslims	13,5	4,8	Luxembourg non-Muslims	11,8	13,5	Luxembourg implied discrimination	1,7	-8,7	-10,4

(Continued)

	low trust in the legal system 2002	low trust in the legal system 2004		low trust in the legal system 2002	low trust in the legal system 2004		low trust in the legal system 2002	low trust in the legal system 2004	DYN relative discrimination
Netherlands Muslims	17,5	22,2	Netherlands non-Muslims	17,4	16,9	Netherlands implied discrimination	0,1	5,3	5,2
Norway Muslims	0	19,1	Norway non-Muslims	11,8	10,8	Norway implied discrimination	-11,8	8,3	20,1
Slovenia Muslims	58,7	60	Slovenia non-Muslims	40,9	47,3	Slovenia implied discrimination	17,8	12,7	-5,1
Spain Muslims	62,5	42,9	Spain non-Muslims	34,6	27,4	Spain implied discrimination	27,9	15,5	-12,4
Sweden Muslims	21,7	30,8	Sweden non-Muslims	12,4	16	Sweden implied discrimination	9,3	14,8	5,5
Switzerland Muslims	0	17,9	Switzerland non-Muslims	9,9	10,4	Switzerland implied discrimination	-9,9	7,5	17,4
UK Muslims	14,3	11,1	UK non-Muslims	23,1	23	UK implied discrimination	-8,8	-11,9	-3,1
Austria Muslims	33,3	39,2	Austria non-Muslims	9,6	11,5	Austria implied discrimination	23,7	27,7	4
Belgium Muslims	13,5	20,6	Belgium non-Muslims	13,1	14,2	Belgium implied discrimination	0,4	6,4	6
Denmark Muslims	9	11,1	Denmark non-Muslims	2,4	2,1	Denmark implied discrimination	6,6	9	2,4
France Muslims	22,9		France non-Muslims	10,8		France implied discrimination	12,1		
Germany Muslims	19,4	14,3	Germany non-Muslims	6,5	7,2	Germany implied discrimination	12,9	7,1	-5,8

(Continued)

	low trust in the police 2002	low trust in the police 2004		low trust in the police 2002	low trust in the police 2004		low trust in the police 2002	low trust in the police 2004	DYN relative discrimination
Greece Muslims	11,5	5,8	Greece non-Muslims	15,6	15,9	Greece implied discrimination	-4,1	-10,1	-6
Israel Muslims	26,8		Israel non-Muslims	14,8		Israel implied discrimination	12		
Luxem-bourg Muslims	16	12,6	Luxem-bourg non-Muslims	9,8	10,3	Luxem-bourg implied discrimination	6,2	2,3	-3,9
Nether-lands Muslims	22,5	23	Nether-lands non-Muslims	11,4	9,4	Nether-lands implied discrimination	11,1	13,6	2,5
Norway Muslims	20	23,9	Norway non-Muslims	5,8	6,4	Norway implied discrimination	14,2	17,5	3,3
Slovenia Muslims	42,2	80	Slovenia non-Muslims	28,9	32,2	Slovenia implied discrimination	13,3	47,8	34,5
Spain Muslims	37,5	20	Spain non-Muslims	17,1	12,3	Spain implied discrimination	20,4	7,7	-12,7
Sweden Muslims	16,7	13,4	Sweden non-Muslims	6,8	10,1	Sweden implied discrimination	9,9	3,3	-6,6
Switzer-land Muslims	0	6,4	Switzer-land non-Muslims	4,7	5	Switzerland implied discrimination	-4,7	1,4	6,1
UK Muslims	17,2	10,5	UK non-Muslims	12,7	12,8	UK implied discrimination	4,5	-2,3	-6,8

(Continued)

	low trust in the way democracy works in the country 2002	low trust in the way democracy works in the country 2004		low trust in the way democracy works in the country 2002	low trust in the way democracy works in the country 2004		low trust in the way democracy works in the country 2002	low trust in the way democracy works in the country 2004	DYN relative discrimination
Austria Muslims	19,1	4,8	Austria non-Muslims	18,5	12,4	Austria implied discrimination	0,6	-7,6	-8,2
Belgium Muslims	2,9	14,3	Belgium non-Muslims	14	16,8	Belgium implied discrimination	-11,1	-2,5	8,6
Denmark Muslims	0	12,6	Denmark non-Muslims	2,7	4,8	Denmark implied discrimination	-2,7	7,8	10,5
France Muslims	15,3		France non-Muslims	22,3		France implied discrimination	-7		
Germany Muslims	14	11,6	Germany non-Muslims	20,6	20,4	Germany implied discrimination	-6,6	-8,8	-2,2
Greece Muslims	18,5	0	Greece non-Muslims	20,8	11	Greece implied discrimination	-2,3	-11	-8,7
Israel Muslims	49,3		Israel non-Muslims	25,7		Israel implied discrimination	23,6		
Luxembourg Muslims	20,9	4,8	Luxembourg non-Muslims	5,9	5,9	Luxembourg implied discrimination	15	-1,1	-16,1
Netherlands Muslims	25,6	28,5	Netherlands non-Muslims	7,4	11,5	Netherlands implied discrimination	18,2	17	-1,2

(Continued)

	low trust in the way democracy works in the country 2002	low trust in the way democracy works in the country 2004		low trust in the way democracy works in the country 2002	low trust in the way democracy works in the country 2004		low trust in the way democracy works in the country 2002	low trust in the way democracy works in the country 2004	DYN relative discrimination
Norway Muslims	15	0	Norway non-Muslims	7,5	10	Norway implied discrimination	7,5	-10	-17,5
Slovenia Muslims	27,8	42,9	Slovenia non-Muslims	36,2	31,3	Slovenia implied discrimination	-8,4	11,6	20
Spain Muslims	42,9	9,5	Spain non-Muslims	11,9	10,3	Spain implied discrimination	31	-0,8	-31,8
Sweden Muslims	4,2	7,1	Sweden non-Muslims	10,2	15,6	Sweden implied discrimination	-6	-8,5	-2,5
Switzerland Muslims	9,1	7,2	Switzerland non-Muslims	6,6	6,5	Switzerland implied discrimination	2,5	0,7	-1,8
UK Muslims	17,6	17,4	UK non-Muslims	22,7	22,5	UK implied discrimination	-5,1	-5,1	0
Austria Muslims	36,7	46,5	Austria non-Muslims	18,3	12	Austria implied discrimination	18,4	34,5	16,1
Belgium Muslims	26,4	46,5	Belgium non-Muslims	15,4	21,9	Belgium implied discrimination	11	24,6	13,6
Denmark Muslims	19	25,1	Denmark non-Muslims	5,1	3,9	Denmark implied discrimination	13,9	21,2	7,3
France Muslims	79,6		France non-Muslims	44		France implied discrimination	35,6		
Germany Muslims	28,1	47,7	Germany non-Muslims	10,7	14,8	Germany implied discrimination	17,4	32,9	15,5

(Continued)

	very difficult on present income + difficult on present income, 2002	very difficult on present income + difficult on present income, 2004		very difficult on present income + difficult on present income, 2002	very difficult on present income + difficult on present income, 2004		very difficult on present income + difficult on present income, 2002	very difficult on present income + difficult on present income, 2004	DYN relative discrimination
Greece Muslims	80,2	82,8	Greece non-Muslims	51,9	50,4	Greece implied discrimination	28,3	32,4	4,1
Israel Muslims	47,4		Israel non-Muslims	39,5		Israel implied discrimination	7,9		
Luxembourg Muslims	38,4	47,8	Luxembourg non-Muslims	9,7	11,3	Luxembourg implied discrimination	28,7	36,5	7,8
Netherlands Muslims	30,8	53,6	Netherlands non-Muslims	9,6	12,9	Netherlands implied discrimination	21,2	40,7	19,5
Norway Muslims	35	27,3	Norway non-Muslims	7,7	9,2	Norway implied discrimination	27,3	18,1	-9,2
Slovenia Muslims	21,1	10	Slovenia non-Muslims	17,4	14,1	Slovenia implied discrimination	3,7	-4,1	-7,8
Spain Muslims	66,6	64	Spain non-Muslims	21,8	18	Spain implied discrimination	44,8	46	1,2
Sweden Muslims	26,1	28,6	Sweden non-Muslims	8,7	8,6	Sweden implied discrimination	17,4	20	2,6
Switzerland Muslims	7,7	56,6	Switzerland non-Muslims	8,2	12,1	Switzerland implied discrimination	-0,5	44,5	45
UK Muslims	27,8	27,1	UK non-Muslims	12,2	17	UK implied discrimination	15,6	10,1	-5,5

Source: calculated by Christian Bischof, Tomaz Kastrun, Karl Mueller and the author from the data of the ESS, available at http://www.europeansocialsurvey.org/

7. THE LISBON PROCESS, EUROPEAN NEIGHBORHOOD POLICY AND POVERTY IN TERMS OF THE EU-25 WIDE NEW POVERTY CRITERION

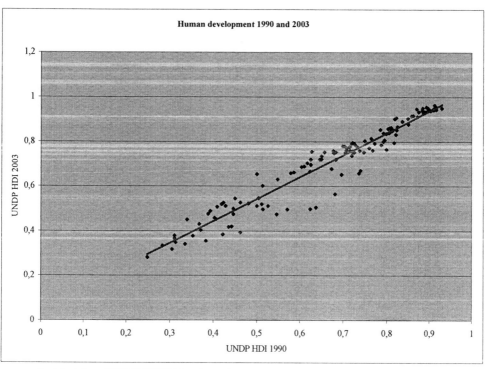

Source: calculated from UNDP (2005) by the author.

Country	Residual HDI 2003 from predicted HDI (regression HDI 1990->HDI 2003)	HDI 1990	HDI 2003	World rank in terms of social development (residual measure of increments in the UNDP HDI)
Ireland	0,0379681	0,87	0,946	24
Luxembourg	0,0270821	0,884	0,949	38
United Kingdom	0,0180739	0,883	0,939	48
Portugal	0,0167972	0,849	0,904	49
Cyprus	0,0166914	0,836	0,891	50
Hungary	0,0164554	0,807	0,862	51
Poland	0,0164228	0,803	0,858	52
Sweden	0,0141878	0,897	0,949	57
Norway	0,0133099	0,912	0,963	59
Belgium	0,0082041	0,899	0,945	63
Italy	0,0071227	0,889	0,934	66
Denmark	0,005196	0,898	0,941	68
Austria	0,0041634	0,894	0,936	72
Germany	0,0041146	0,888	0,93	73

(Continued)

Country	Residual HDI 2003 from predicted HDI (regression HDI 1990->HDI 2003)	HDI 1990	HDI 2003	World rank in terms of social development (residual measure of increments in the UNDP HDI)
Spain	0,0040983	0,886	0,928	74
Malta	0,0036019	0,825	0,867	76
Iceland	0,0033343	0,915	0,956	77
Finland	0,0022204	0,901	0,941	78
Greece	0,0019844	0,872	0,912	80
Estonia	0,0005124	0,814	0,853	82
Switzerland	-0,000706	0,91	0,947	83
Latvia	-0,00161	0,799	0,836	87
Netherlands	-0,002723	0,908	0,943	90
France	-0,002763	0,903	0,938	91
Lithuania	-0,009414	0,823	0,852	97
Romania	-0,018829	0,772	0,792	106
Bulgaria	-0,025642	0,795	0,808	108
Other states				
China	0,0879905	0,627	0,755	2
Tunisia	0,0562347	0,657	0,753	7
India	0,0480627	0,513	0,602	11
Lebanon	0,0423974	0,677	0,759	19
Morocco	0,0423476	0,548	0,631	21
Egypt	0,0395999	0,579	0,659	23
Albania	0,037609	0,703	0,78	25
Syrian Arab Republic	0,0351451	0,646	0,721	28
Algeria	0,0331695	0,649	0,722	30
Turkey	0,0324056	0,678	0,75	31
Jordan	0,0304462	0,683	0,753	34
Israel	0,0188705	0,858	0,915	46
Croatia	-0,003553	0,806	0,841	92
Japan	-0,005698	0,911	0,943	94
United States	-0,009658	0,916	0,944	98
Armenia	-0,017114	0,737	0,759	103
Canada	-0,017552	0,929	0,949	105
Belarus	-0,039707	0,787	0,786	118
Kazakhstan	-0,04487	0,767	0,761	119
Russian Federation	-0,060463	0,817	0,795	123

(Continued)

Country	Residual HDI 2003 from predicted HDI (regression HDI 1990->HDI 2003)	HDI 1990	HDI 2003	World rank in terms of social development (residual measure of increments in the UNDP HDI)
Ukraine	-0,07161	0,799	0,766	126
Moldova, Rep, of	-0,107098	0,739	0,671	129

Source: calculated from UNDP (2005) by the author.

The (partial) European incapacity to increase the Muslim development index well explains the unsatisfactory human development performance, 1990 – 2003; see also the data from the Table Appendix 4 above and Table 6a.

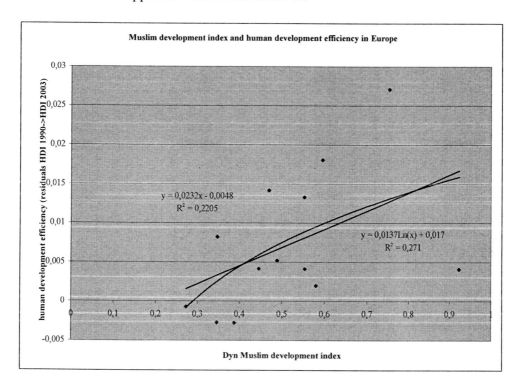

8. THE NEW INDEX OF POVERTY IN THE ENLARGED EU-25, BASED ON THE CRITERION: POVERTY AS DEFINED BY THE PERCENTAGE OF PEOPLE WHOSE INCOME IS 60 % OR LESS THE EU-25 WIDE MEAN INCOME

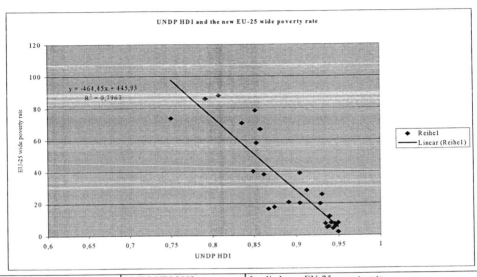

	UNDP HDI 2003	Implied new EU-25 poverty rate y = -464,45*UNDP HDI + 445,93; R2 = 0,7967
Turkey	0,75	97,59
Tunisia	0,753	96,2
Jordan	0,753	96,2
China	0,755	95,27
Lebanon	0,759	93,41
Armenia	0,759	93,41
Kazakhstan	0,761	92,48
Ukraine	0,766	90,16
Albania	0,78	83,66
Belarus	0,786	80,87
Romania	0,792	78,09
Russian Federation	0,795	76,69
Bulgaria	0,808	70,65
Latvia	0,836	57,65
Croatia	0,841	55,33
Lithuania	0,852	50,22

(Continued)

	UNDP HDI 2003	Implied new EU-25 poverty rate y = -464,45*UNDP HDI + 445,93; R2 = 0,7967
Estonia	0,853	49,75
Poland	0,858	47,43
Hungary	0,862	45,57
Malta	0,867	43,25
Cyprus	0,891	32,11
Portugal	0,904	26,07
Greece	0,912	22,35
Israel	0,915	20,96
Spain	0,928	14,92
Germany	0,93	13,99
Italy	0,934	12,13
Austria	0,936	11,2
France	0,938	10,28
United Kingdom	0,939	9,81
Denmark	0,941	8,88
Finland	0,941	8,88
Netherlands	0,943	7,95
Japan	0,943	7,95
United States	*0,944*	*7,49*
Belgium	0,945	7,02
Ireland	0,946	6,56
Switzerland	0,947	6,1
Luxembourg	0,949	5,17
Sweden	0,949	5,17
Canada	0,949	5,17
Iceland	0,956	1,92

9. FURTHER PROPERTIES OF THE NEW POVERTY INDEX, BASED ON THE EU-25 WIDE MEDIAN INCOME

	% poor re EU25 median	UNDP HDI	quintile ratio	comparative price level (based on 1/ERDI)	GDP US $	GDP PPP $
Sweden	2	0,949	4	1,258765	301,6	239,6
Netherlands	4,4	0,943	5,1	1,073452	511,5	476,5
Austria	5	0,936	4,7	1,039425	253,1	243,5
France	5,4	0,938	5,6	1,062636	1757,6	1654
Ireland	5,9	0,946	6,1	1,019907	153,7	150,7
Italy	7,3	0,934	6,5	0,939231	1468,3	1563,3
Belgium	7,3	0,945	4,5	1,026871	301,9	294
Luxembourg	7,7	0,949	3,7	0,949821	26,5	27,9
Finland	7,7	0,941	3,8	1,124306	161,9	144
Denmark	7,9	0,941	4,3	1,250147	211,9	169,5
UK	11,9	0,939	7,2	1,114429	1794,9	1610,6
Malta	16,7	0,867	4,6	0,7	4,9	7
Czech Rep	17,8	0,874	3,5	0,537448	89,7	166,9
Spain	19,8	0,928	5,4	0,911333	838,7	920,3
Slovenia	20,2	0,904	3,9	0,725131	27,7	38,2
Cyprus	20,8	0,891	4,1	0,797203	11,4	14,3
Germany	25,5	0,93	4,3	1,048974	2403,2	2291
Greece	28,2	0,912	6,2	0,782016	172,2	220,2
Hungary	38,4	0,862	3,8	0,559919	82,7	147,7
Portugal	39,1	0,904	8	0,7813	147,9	189,3
Slovakia	40,3	0,849	4	0,447043	32,5	72,7
Estonia	58,1	0,853	7,2	0,497268	9,1	18,3
Poland	66,6	0,858	5,5	0,482283	209,6	434,6
Latvia	70,5	0,836	5,6	0,466387	11,1	23,8
Turkey	73,5	0,75	7,7	0,501984	240,4	478,9
Lithuania	78,5	0,852	5,1	0,450495	18,2	40,4
Romania	85,9	0,792	5,2	0,360303	57	158,2
Bulgaria	88	0,808	5,8	0,328926	19,9	60,5

Ex definition, the comparative price level in the US = 1.0, because GDP $ = GDP PPP $ in that country

% poor re EU25 median	UNDP HDI	quintile ratio	comparative price level (1/ERDI)	constant
	-39,69438	3,260533	-256,3087	274,4523
	18,21282	1,885556	98,64139	78,74213
	0,84096	11,92869		
	42,30157	24		
	18057,73	3415,047		
t-test	-2,179474	1,729216	-2,598389	3,485457
t-test and direction of influence^2	4,750109	2,990187	6,751623	12,14841
t-test and direction of influence^0,5	2,179474	1,729216	2,598389	3,485457
degrees of freedom	24	24	24	24
error probability	0,03934	0,096615	0,015762	0,00191
F equation	42,30157	42,30157	42,30157	42,30157
error probability, entire equation	9,75E-10	9,75E-10	9,75E-10	9,75E-10
% poor re country median	UNDP HDI	quintile ratio	comparative price level (1/ERDI)	constant
	3,992491	1,220667	2,381668	8,547088
	7,618334	0,788719	41,2612	32,93744
	0,131813	4,989711		
	1,214608	24		
	90,7211	597,5332		
t-test	0,524064	1,547658	0,057722	0,259495
t-test and direction of influence^2	0,274643	2,395246	0,003332	0,067337
t-test and direction of influence^0,5	0,524064	1,547658	0,057722	0,259495
degrees of freedom	24	24	24	24
error probability	0,605041	*0,134791*	0,954448	0,797467
F equation	1,214608	1,214608	1,214608	1,214608
error probability, entire equation	0,325855	0,325855	0,325855	0,325855

Legend: Our entire EXCEL 7.0 calculations are from UNDP and other data sources, quoted above. As in all EXCEL 7.0 outprints, first row: un-standardized regression coefficients, second row: standard errors, second last row: t-Test and direction of the influence. The values immediately below the standard errors are R^2 (third row, left side entry), F, and degrees of freedom (fourth row). Below that: ss $_{reg}$, ss $_{resid}$, i.e. the sum of squares of the regression and the sum of squares of the residuals. The right-hand entry in the third row is the standard error of the estimate y.

10. ESTIMATING THE HUMAN DEVELOPMENT INDEX FOR THE MUSLIM COMMUNITIES IN EUROPE FROM ESS DATA

Since there are no direct data available, which allow the calculation of the UNDP Human Development Index for the Muslim communities in Europe, we simply used the data of Table 10 to calculate a linear estimate of the UNDP HDI, based on the available ESS data on income deficit groups.

This calculation might be a very crude one, but it provides at least an informed guess about the assumed human development indices of the Muslim communities in Europe.

First we estimate the relationship between the percentage of income deficit groups per total population according to the ESS and the UNDP HDI:

	income deficit groups per total population	UNDP HDI as a proxy for the Lisbon process
Austria	12	0,936
Belgium	21,9	0,945
Czech	49,3	0,874
Denmark	3,9	0,941
Estonia	52,2	0,853
Finland	13,4	0,941
France	44	0,938
Germany	14,8	0,93
Greece	50,4	0,912
Hungary	49,3	0,862
Iceland	8	0,956
Ireland	10,5	0,946
Italy	17	0,934
Luxembourg	11,3	0,949
Netherlands	12,9	0,943
Norway	9,2	0,963
Poland	41	0,858
Portugal	40	0,904
Slovakia	54,8	0,849
Slovenia	14,1	0,904
Spain	18	0,928
Sweden	8,6	0,949
Switzerland	12,1	0,947
Ukraine	79,5	0,766
United Kingdom	17	0,939

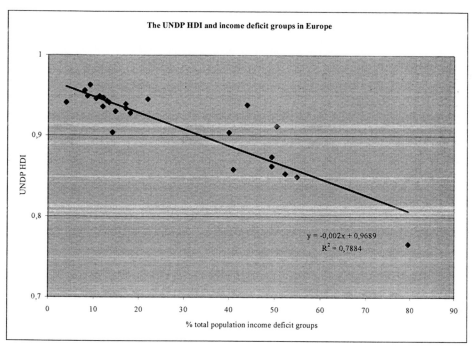

This yields the following estimates for the UNDP HDI for the Muslim communities in Europe:

	% of total Muslim population belonging to income deficit groups	assumed UNDP HDI y = -0,002x + 0,9689; R2 = 0,7884
Greece Muslims	82,8	0,8033
France Muslims	79,6	0,8097
Spain Muslims	64	0,8409
Switzerland Muslims	56,6	0,8557
Netherlands Muslims	53,6	0,8617
Luxembourg Muslims	47,8	0,8733
Germany Muslims	47,7	0,8735
Austria Muslims	46,5	0,8759
Belgium Muslims	46,5	0,8759
Sweden Muslims	28,6	0,9117
Norway Muslims	27,3	0,9143
United Kingdom Muslims	27,1	0,9147
Denmark Muslims	25,1	0,9187
Slovenia Muslims	10	0,9489

Our second estimate is based on the percentages of the political center per total population. This estimate yields the following results:

	center+center left+center right	UNDP HDI as a proxy for the Lisbon process
Austria	78,9	0,936
Belgium	80,4	0,945
Czech	64	0,874
Denmark	76,9	0,941
Estonia	80,1	0,853
Finland	73,3	0,941
France	70,7	0,938
Germany	82,3	0,93
Greece	69,2	0,912
Hungary	72,8	0,862
Iceland	77,3	0,956
Ireland	85,1	0,946
Italy	71,8	0,934
Luxembourg	77,7	0,949
Netherlands	78,3	0,943
Norway	77,9	0,963
Poland	71,8	0,858
Portugal	73,8	0,904
Slovakia	69,7	0,849
Slovenia	71,9	0,904
Spain	72,2	0,928
Sweden	71,7	0,949
Switzerland	80,9	0,947
Ukraine	64	0,766
United Kingdom	85,4	0,939

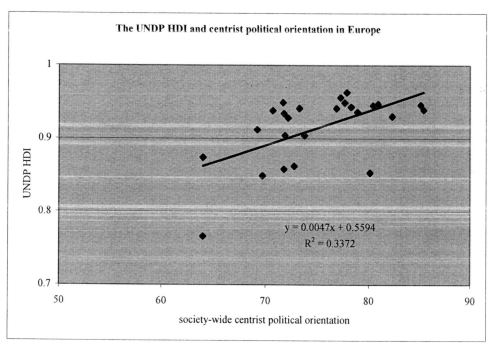

The relationship is again quite strong, explaining over 1/3 of the variance of the UNDP HDI. The estimates for the UNDP HDI are the following:

	% of the Muslim population oriented towards the political center	assumed UNDP HDI $y = 0{,}0047x + 0{,}5594$; $R2 = 0{,}3372$
Spain	50,0	0,7944
Belgium	57,2	0,82824
Luxembourg	57,2	0,82824
France	58,7	0,83529
Denmark	71,4	0,89498
Switzerland	74,9	0,91143
Netherlands	76,2	0,91754
Germany	83,3	0,95091
Sweden	83,3	0,95091
Austria	85,7	0,96219
Greece	85,7	0,96219
Norway	85,7	0,96219
Slovenia	87,5	0,97065
United Kingdom	87,5	0,97065

Working with estimate (1) we are confronted with the following table of world-wide Human Development:

	Human development index 2003
Norway	0,963
Iceland	0,956
Australia	0,955
Luxembourg	0,949
Canada	0,949
Sweden	0,949
Slovenia Muslims	*0,949*
Switzerland	0,947
Ireland	0,946
Belgium	0,945
United States	0,944
Japan	0,943
Netherlands	0,943
Finland	0,941
Denmark	0,941
United Kingdom	0,939
France	0,938
Austria	0,936
Italy	0,934
New Zealand	0,933
Germany	0,93
Spain	0,928
Denmark Muslims	*0,919*
Hong Kong, China (SAR)	0,916
Israel	0,915
United Kingdom Muslims	*0,915*
Norway Muslims	*0,914*
Greece	0,912
Sweden Muslims	*0,912*
Singapore	0,907
Slovenia	0,904
Portugal	0,904
Korea, Rep, of	0,901
Cyprus	0,891
Barbados	0,878
Austria Muslims	*0,876*
Belgium Muslims	*0,876*
Czech Republic	0,874
Germany Muslims	*0,874*

(Continued)

	Human development index 2003
Luxembourg Muslims	*0,873*
Malta	0,867
Brunei Darussalam	0,866
Argentina	0,863
Hungary	0,862
Netherlands Muslims	*0,862*
Poland	0,858
Switzerland Muslims	*0,856*
Chile	0,854
Estonia	0,853
Lithuania	0,852
Qatar	0,849
United Arab Emirates	0,849
Slovakia	0,849
Bahrain	0,846
Kuwait	0,844
Croatia	0,841
Spain Muslims	*0,841*
Uruguay	0,84
Costa Rica	0,838
Latvia	0,836
Saint Kitts and Nevis	0,834
Bahamas	0,832
Seychelles	0,821
Cuba	0,817
Mexico	0,814
Tonga	0,81
France Muslims	*0,810*
Bulgaria	0,808
Panama	0,804
Greece Muslims	*0,803*
Trinidad and Tobago	0,801
Libyan Arab Jamahiriya	0,799
Macedonia, TFYR	0,797
Antigua and Barbuda	0,797
Malaysia	0,796
Russian Federation	0,795
Brazil	0,792
Romania	0,792
Mauritius	0,791

(Continued)

	Human development index 2003
Grenada	0,787
Belarus	0,786
Bosnia and Herzegovina	0,786
Colombia	0,785
Dominica	0,783
Oman	0,781
Albania	0,78
Thailand	0,778
Samoa (Western)	0,776
Venezuela	0,772
Saint Lucia	0,772
Saudi Arabia	0,772
Ukraine	0,766
Peru	0,762
Kazakhstan	0,761
Lebanon	0,759
Ecuador	0,759
Armenia	0,759
Philippines	0,758
China	0,755
Suriname	0,755
Saint Vincent and the Grenadines	0,755
Paraguay	0,755
Tunisia	0,753
Jordan	0,753
Belize	0,753
Fiji	0,752
Sri Lanka	0,751
Turkey	0,750

11. The UNDP HDI (Human Development Index) and Religious Service Attendance in Different Nations of the World and Among the European Muslim Communities

	Human Development Index 2003	Religious service attendance rate	ex USSR
Russian Federation	0,795	0,02	yes
Estonia	0,853	0,04	yes
Latvia	0,836	0,05	yes
Belarus	0,786	0,06	yes
Armenia	0,759	0,08	yes
Georgia	0,732	0,1	yes
Moldova, Rep, of	0,671	0,1	yes
Ukraine	0,766	0,1	yes
Lithuania	0,852	0,16	yes
Japan	0,943	0,03	no
Finland	0,941	0,04	no
Iceland	0,956	0,04	no
Sweden	0,949	0,04	no
Denmark	0,941	0,05	no
Norway	0,963	0,05	no
Azerbaijan	0,729	0,06	no
China	0,755	0,09	no
Bulgaria	0,808	0,1	no
Czech Republic	0,874	0,14	no
Korea, Rep, of	0,901	0,14	no
Australia	0,955	0,16	no
Switzerland	0,947	0,16	no
Romania	0,792	0,2	no
France	0,938	0,21	no
Hungary	0,862	0,21	no
Croatia	0,841	0,22	no
Argentina	0,863	0,25	no
Chile	0,854	0,25	no
Spain	0,928	0,25	no
United Kingdom	0,939	0,27	no
Austria	0,936	0,3	no
Uruguay	0,84	0,31	no
Venezuela	0,772	0,31	no
Netherlands	0,943	0,35	no

(Continued)

	HDI 2003	Religious service attendance	ex USSR
Brazil	0,792	0,36	no
Canada	0,949	0,38	no
India	0,602	0,42	no
Peru	0,762	0,43	no
Turkey	0,75	0,43	no
Belgium	0,945	0,44	no
United States	0,944	0,44	no
Italy	0,934	0,45	no
Mexico	0,814	0,46	no
Portugal	0,904	0,47	no
Slovakia	0,849	0,47	no
Poland	0,858	0,55	no
South Africa	0,658	0,56	no
Philippines	0,758	0,68	no
Ireland	0,946	0,84	no
Nigeria	0,453	0,89	no
Austria Muslims	0,876	14,3	no
Belgium Muslims	0,876	22,4	no
Denmark Muslims	0,919	28,6	no
France Muslims	0,81	8,7	no
Germany Muslims	0,874	38,1	no
Greece Muslims	0,803	42,9	no
Luxembourg Muslims	0,873	0	no
Netherlands Muslims	0,862	19	no
Norway Muslims	0,914	28,6	no
Slovenia Muslims	0,949	12,5	no
Spain Muslims	0,841	20	no
Sweden Muslims	0,912	0	no
Switzerland Muslims	0,856	20,8	no
United Kingdom Muslims	0,915	40	no

Source: our own calculations from ESS, 2002 and 2004, and nationmaster.com based on world value survey[1].

---

[1] Some statistics on Muslim communities in the text also drew from "Islamicweb" at *http://islamicweb.com/begin/population.htm* . For Malta, we implied a community of 0.5 % Muslims, for Cyprus, where the last population census with religious data took place only before the events of the 1970s, we equally assumed a percentage of 0.5 %.

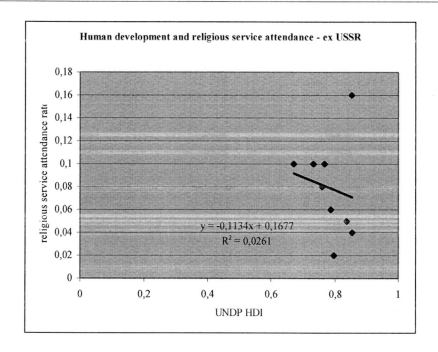

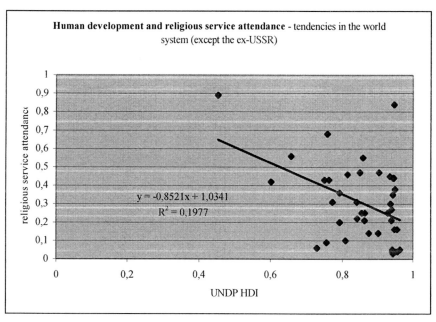

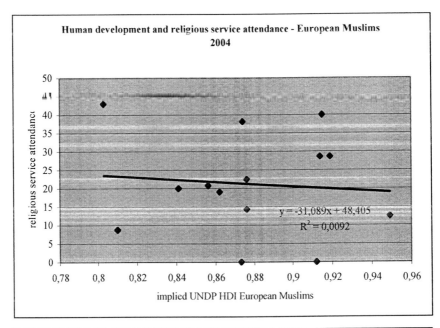

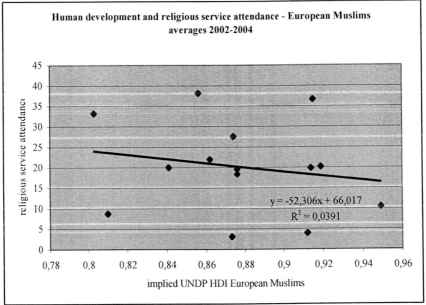

LITERATURE AND DATA SOURCES

Internet Sources:

*http://www.lalisio.com/members/m_TAUSCH/publications/114986208075/114986228444/?u
se_session=Trueandbrowser_type=Explorerand-C=andlanguage=en*
http://www.cgdev.org/content/expert/detail/2699/

Sources provided by the ILO, the UTIP project at the University of Texas, and the World
Bank were used in this essay. These analyses of the dynamics in the world system
calculated the time series correlations of globalization, economic growth (Global
Development Network Growth Database, William Easterly and Mirvat Sewadeh, World
Bank), unemployment (Laborsta ILO), and inequality (UTIP, University of Texas
Inequality Project, Theil indices of inequality, based on wages in 21 economic sectors)
since 1980.

http://www.worldbank.org/research/growth/GDNdata.htm
http://laborsta.ilo.org/
http://utip.gov.utexas.edu/

Armstrong K. (1992), *'Muhammad: a biography of the prophet'* San Francisco, Calif.: Harper
SanFrancisco.
Armstrong K. (2006), *'Muhammad: a prophet for our time'* New York: Atlas
Books/HarperCollins
Aydin H. et al. (2003), *'"Euro-Islam". Das neue Islamverständnis der Muslime in der
Migration".* Stiftung Zentrum für Türkeistudien, Institut an der Universität Duisburg-
Essen. Available at: *http://www.renner-institut.at/download/texte/euroisla.pdf*
BM.I .SIAK (2006), *'Perspektiven und Herausforderungen in der Integration muslimischer
MitbürgerInnen in Österreich'* Federal Ministry of the Interior, Republic of Austria,
available at: *http://www.bmi.gv.at/downloadarea/asyl_fremdenwesen/Perspektiven
_Herausforderungen.pdf*
Boff L. (1985), *'Church, charism and power: liberation theology and the institutional
church'.* London: SCM Press.
Boff L. (2005), *'Global civilization: challenges to society and to Christianity.'* London;
Oakville : Equinox Publishing
Dennis I. and Guio A. C. (2004), 'Armut und soziale Ausgrenzung in der EU' Statistik kurz
gefasst, Eurostat, 16, available at: *http://www.eds-destatis.de/de/downloads/sif/nk_04*

_16.pdfsearch=%22Armut%20und%20soziale%20Ausgrenzung%20in%20der%20EU%2 0Dennis%20Guio%22

Dennis I. and Guio A. C. (2004), 'Monetary poverty in the new Member States and Candidate Countries' Statistik kurz gefasst, Eurostat, 12, available at: *www.eustatistics.gov uk/Download.asp?KS-NK-04-012-EN tcm90-17101.pdf*

Dittrich M. (2006), *'Muslims in Europe: addressing the challenges of radicalisation'*. European Policy Centre in strategic partnership with the King Baudouin Foundation and the Comagnia di San Paolo, Brussels, available at *http://www.theepc.be /TEWN/pdf/602431467_EPC%20Working%20Paper%2023%20Muslims%20in%20Euro pe.pdf*

Erdenir B. (2006), 'The Future of Europe: Islamophobia?' Secretariat General for EU Affairs (EUSG) of Turkey, available at: http://www.turkishpolicy.com/default.asp?show=fall_ 2005_erdenir (Turkish Policy Quarterly, 2006).

European Social Survey (2006), Data materials, freely available from: *http:// www.europeansocialsurvey.org/*

European Stability Initiative (2006), *'Islamic Calvinists. Change and Conservatism in Central Anatolia'*. European Stability Initiative, Berlin, Brussels, Istanbul, available at: *http://www.esiweb.org/*

Fahey T. Et al. (2005), 'First European Quality of Life Survey: Income inequalities and deprivation' European Foundation for the Improvement of Living and Wokring Conditions, available at: *http://www.eurofound.eu.int/pubdocs/2005/93/en/1/ef0593en.pdf*

Inglehart R. and Norris P. (2003), 'The True Clash of Civilizations' *Foreign Policy,* March/April 2003, available at: *http://www. globalpolicy. org/globaliz/cultural /2003/0304clash.htm*

Inglehart R. and Norris P. (2004), *'Sacred and Secular: Religion and Politics Worldwide (Cambridge Studies in Social Theory, Religion and Politics) (Paperback)'*. Cambridge and New York: Cambridge University Press.

Muenz R. (2006), *"Population Change and the Impact of Demographic Aging: Consequences and Policy Options for Europe"* International Conference on Cultural and Political Conditions for the Reform and Modernisation of Social Models in Europe and the U.S., Vienna, May 19-20, 2006, Institute for Human Sciences, Vienna

Olson M. (1982), *'The Rise and Decline of Nations'* New Haven and London: Yale University Press.

Olson M. (1986), 'A Theory of the Incentives Facing Political Organizations. Neo - Corporatism and the Hegemonic State' *International Political Science Review,* 7, 2, April: 165 - 89.

Olson M. (1987), 'Ideology and Economic Growth' in *'The Legacy of Reaganomics. Prospects for Long - term Growth'* (Hulten Ch.R. and Sawhill I.V. (Eds.)), pp. 229 - 251, Washington D.C.: The Urban Institute Press.

PEW Research Center for the People and the Press (2006), "The Great Divide: How Westerners and Muslims View Each Other. Europe's Muslims More Moderate" PEW, Washington D.C.: *http://pewglobal.org/reports/display.php?ReportID=253* (June 22, 2006)

Pipes D. (2002), 'God and Mammon: Does Poverty Cause Militant Islam? *The National Interest,* Winter 2002, available at: *http://www.danielpipes.org/article/104*

Rabasa A. M. et al. (2006), *"The Muslim World after 9/11. Prepared for the United States Air Force"*. Rand Corporation, Santa Monica, California, Rand Project Air Force, available at: *http://www.rand.org/pubs/research_briefs/2005/RAND_RB151.pdf*

Sapir A. (2005a), ,Globalisation and the Reform of European Social Models'. Brussels, BRUEGEL Institute (Background document for the presentation at ECOFIN Informal Meeting in Manchester, 9 September 2005), available at: *http://www.bruegel.org /Repositories/Documents/publications/working_papers/SapirPaper080905.pdf*.

Sapir A. (2005b), ,Globalisation and the Reform of European Social Models' Brussels, BRUEGEL Institute, bruegel policy brief, 01, November (restricted).

Sapir A. et al. (2004), *"An agenda for a growing Europe. Making the EU economic system deliver"* available at: *http://www.euractiv.com/ndbtext/innovation/sapirreport.pdf*

Savage T. M. (2004), 'Europe and Islam: Crescent Waxing, Cultures Clashing' The Washington Quarterly, Summer, 27, 3: 25-50, available at: *http://www.twq.com/04summer/docs/04summer_savage.pdfsearch=%22crescent%20wax ing%20savage%22*

Schmitt J. and Zipperer B. (2006), 'Is the U.S. a Good Model for Reducing Social Exclusion in Europe?' Center for Economic and Policy Research, Washington D.C., available at: *http://www.cepr.net/publications/social_exclusion_2006_08.pdfsearch=%22Is%20the%2 0US%20a%20Godd%20Model%20for%20Reducing%20Social%20Exclusion%20in%20 Europe%20%22Is%20the%20U.S.%20a%20Good%20Model%20for%20Reducing%20S ocial%20Exclusion%20in%20Europe%22%22*

Tausch A. (2002, with Andreas Mueller et al. (Eds.)), *'Global Capitalism, Liberation Theology and the Social Sciences. An Analysis of the Contradictions of Modernity at the Turn of the Millenium'*. Hauppauge, New York: Nova Science Publishers

Tausch A. (2001, with Gernot Köhler) *Global Keynesianism: Unequal exchange and global exploitation.* Huntington NY, Nova Science. ISBN 1-59033-002-1. Paperback edition 2001

Tausch A. (2001, with Peter Herrmann) *Globalization and European Integration.* Huntington NY, Nova Science. ISBN: 1-560729295.

Tausch A. (2003) 'The European Union: Global Challenge or Global Governance? 14 World System Hypotheses and Two Scenarios on the Future of the Union' in *'Globalization: Critical Perspectives'* (Gernot Kohler and Emilio José Chaves (Editors)), pp. 93 – 197, Hauppauge, New York: Nova Science Publishers

Tausch A. (2003) 'Jevropejskaja perspektiva: po puti k sosdaniju "obshtshevo srjedisemnomorskovo doma" i integrirovaniju polozytelnovo potencjala obshestvjennovo razvitija islamskich stran' in *Evropa,* 4 (9), 2003: 87 – 109, Warsaw, Polish Institute for International Affairs (in Russian language)

Tausch A. (2003) „Social Cohesion, Sustainable Development and Turkey's Accession to the European Union". *Alternatives: Turkish Journal of International Relations,* 2, 1, Spring *http://www.alternativesjournal.net/* and *http://www .alternativesjournal .net/volume2 /number1/tausch.htm*

Tausch A. (2003) Ueber Konvergenz und Ungleichgewicht. *Oesterreichische Monatshefte,* 3: 49 - 56

Tausch A. (2004) 'Die EU-Erweiterung und die soziale Konvergenz. Ein „Working Paper" zur Globalisierung und wachsenden Ungleichheit im neuen und alten Europa' *Studien von Zeitfragen*, ISSN-1619-8417, 38(2): 1 – 185 *http://druckversion.studien-von-zeitfragen.net/Soziale%20Konvergenz%20EU-Erweiterung.pdf*

Tausch A. (2004) 'Europa - groß und mächtig?' In *"Solidarität. Gesellschaft, Gemeinschaft und Individuum in Vergangenheit, Gegenwart und Zukunft"* (Michael Rosecker and Bernhard Müller (Eds)) Wiener Neustadt, Austria: Verein Alltag Verlag, ISBN 3--902282-02-9: pp. 98 - 126

Tausch A. (2004) ‚EU-Erweiterung oder Rekolonisierung des europäischen Ostens? Besprechungsessay zu: Hannes Hofbauer: Osterweiterung' *Zeitschrift fuer Weltgeschichte,* ISSN 1615-2581, 5, 2, Herbst 2004: 113 – 128

Tausch A. (2004) ‚Für immer ausgegrenzt? Neue Studien zur sozialen Lage der Roma in Europa' *Das Juedische Echo,* October 2004, Vol. 53, Tischiri 5765: 147-150, and *Die Zukunft/Akzente,* 06/2004: 35 – 41

Tausch A. (2004) ‚Soziale und regionale Ungleichgewichte, politische Instabilität und die Notwendigkeit von Pensionsreformen im neuen Europa' Schriftenreihe des Zentrums für europäische Studien, Universität Trier, Band 56, ISSN 0948-1141 *http://www.uni-trier.de/zes/schriftenreihe/056.pdf*

Tausch A. (2004) ‚Towards a European Perspective for the Common Mediterranean House and the Positive Development Capability of Islamic Countries' In , *European Neighbourhood Policy: Political, Economic and Social Issues'* (Fulvio Attina and Rosa Rossi (Eds.) Università degli Studi di Catania Facoltà di Scienze Politiche: 145 – 168.

Tausch A. (2004) Ausgegrenzt, aber keine Nomaden. *Die Furche,* 8, 19. Februar 2002: 6

Tausch A. (2004) Bleibt Europa ewig hinten? Über den vom EU-Kommissionspräsidenten Romano Prodi in Auftrag gegebenen Sapir-Bericht. *Die Zukunft,* 2: 11 - 13

Tausch A. (2004) 'Die "Festung Europa" Schleifen' *International. Die Zeitschrift fuer internationale Politik,* 2, 3: 30 – 32

Tausch A. (2004) 'Fuer immer ausgegrenzt?' *International. Die Zeitschrift fuer internationale Politik,* 2, 3: 26 – 29.

Tausch A. (2005) (with Peter Herrmann) *'Dar al Islam. The Mediterranean, the World System and the Wider Europe. Vol. 1: The "Cultural Enlargement" of the EU and Europe's Identity; Vol. 2: The Chain of Peripheries and the New Wider Europe'.* Hauppauge, New York: Nova Science Publishers. Abridged paperback editions 2006 under the title: *"The West, Europe and the Muslim World"* (Vol. 1) and *"Towards a Wider Europe"* (Vol. 2)

Tausch A. (2005) 'A Humanist and Activist for Human Rights. To the Memory of Andre Gunder Frank, February 24, 1929 – April 23, 2005' *Das Jüdische Echo,* 54, Tischri 5766, Oktober 2005: 261 – 263.

Tausch A. (2005) 'Book Review: Michael Mesch and Agnes Streissler (Eds.), US-amerikanisches und Europäisches Modell' in *Evropa,* (5), 2 (15), 2005: 175-185, Warsaw, Polish Institute for International Affairs (in Russian language)

Tausch A. (2005) 'Im Lissabon-Prozess. Die USA und Europa im Vergleich' *Studien von Zeitfragen,* 38, August; available at: *http://www.druckversion.studien-von-zeitfragen.net /Entwicklungsvergleich.pdf*

Tausch A. (2005) ‚Did recent trends in world society make multinational corporations penetration irrelevant? Looking back on Volker Bornschier's development theory in the light of recent evidence'. *Historia Actual On-Line,* 6 Tausch A. (2005), [revista en línea,

Universidad de Cadiz, Espana] Disponible desde Internet en: *http://www.historia-actual.com/hao/Volumes/Volume1/Issue6/esp/v1i6c4.pdf*

Tausch A. (2005) ‚Europe, the Muslim Mediterranean and the End of the era of Global Confrontation’. Alternatives. Turkish Journal of International Relations, Volume 3, Number 4, Winter 2004, available at: *http://www.alternativesjournal .net/volume3 /number4/arno3.pdf*

Tausch A. (2005) ‚Reforming European Pension Systems’. Transcript of the debate at the Conference on “Reforming European pension systems. In memory of Professor Franco Modigliani. 24 and 25 September 2004”, Castle of Schengen, Luxembourg Institute for European and International Studies. Available from the Luxembourg Institute for European and International Studies (LIEIS), at *http://www.ieis.lu/Reports/Reforming% 20European%20Pension%20Systems.pdf*

Tausch A. (2005) ‚Tectonic shifts in the structure of international inequality’. Centro Argentino de Estudios Internacionales, Teoría de las Relaciones Internacionales Working Paper N° 11, Fecha de Publicación: 14/11/05, available at *http://caei.com.ar/es/ programas/teoria/working.htm* also available from: IDEAS, University of Connecticut, at *http://econwpa.wustl.edu/eps/dev/papers/0510/0510009.doc* and from the Global Development Network at *http://www.gdnet.org/middle.php?oid=23 7andzone= docsandaction=docanddoc=10751*

Tausch A. (2005) 'Is Islam really a development blockade? 12 predictors of development, including membership in the Organization of Islamic Conference, and their influence on 14 indicators of development in 109 countries of the world with completely available data'. Ankara Institute for Turkish Policy Studies, ANKAM, *Insight Turkey,* 7, 1, 2005: 124 - 135.

Tausch A. (2005, with Russell A. Berman) „Yet Another reason They Dislike Us. „Europe is rich, but the United States is richer.“ *Hoover Digest,* 2005, 1: 69–73

Tausch A. (2006) ‘On heroes, villains and statisticians’. *The Vienna Institute Monthly Report,* No. 7, July 2006: 20 - 23. Vienna: The Vienna Institute for International Economic Studies (wiiw)

Tausch A. (2006), ‘From the “Washington” towards a “Vienna Consensus”? A quantitative analysis on globalization, development and global governance’. Paper, prepared for the discussion process leading up to the EU-Latin America and Caribbean Summit 2006, May 11, 2006 to May 12, 2006, Vienna, Austria. Centro Argentino de Estudios Internacionales, Buenos Aires, available at: *http://www.caei.com.ar/es/irebooks.htm* (First edition: February 2006, second edition: April 2006). Rapid download also available from: *http://druckversion.studien-von-zeitfragen.net/CAEI_Buenos_ Aires_Vienna _Summit_2nd_edition.pdf* and at the Global Development Network, *http://www.gdnet.org/middle.php?oid=237andzone=docsandaction=docanddoc=10752*

Tausch A. (2006), *‘The City on a Hill? The Latin Americanization of Europe and the Lost Competition with the U.S.A.’* Amsterdam: Rozenberg and Dutch University Press.

Tausch A. (2006), ‘The Lisbon process, re-visited. A reality check of the European social model. Paper, prepared for the International Conference “Economic Relations in the Enlarged EU”. University of Wroclaw, Poland. May 11, 2006 – May 12, 2006. Available at: *http://www.caei.com.ar/es/programas/teoria/16.pdf* Rapid download also available from: *http://druckversion.studien-von-zeitfragen.net/caei_buenos_aires_bolkestein_*

directive.pdf and from the Global Development Network at *http://www.gdnet .org/middle.php?oid=237andzone=docsandaction=docanddoc=10750*

Tausch A. (2006), ,Für Rückkehr der Vernunft in der Türkei-Politik' *Europäische Rundschau*, 34, 1: 121 - 132

Tausch A. (2006, forthcoming, with Almas Heshmati), *'Roadmap to Bangalore? Globalization, the EU's Lisbon Process and the Structures of Global Inequality'* Hauppauge, N.Y.: Nova Science Publishers.

Tausch A. (2006, with Alfonso Galindo Lucas), "La Unión Europea, La "Ciudad en la Colina" y el proceso de Lisboa". Centro Argentino de Estudios Internacionales, Integración Regional Working Paper No 12, Fecha de Publicación: 31/01/06, available at *http://caei.com.ar/es/programas/integracion/working.htm* and at the Global Development Network, *http://www.gdnet.org/middle.php?oid=237andzone=docsandaction=   docan ddoc=10749*

Tausch A. (2006, with Almas Heshmati) 'Turkey and the Lisbon process. A short research note on the position of Turkey on a new "Lisbon Strategy Index" (LSI).' Ankara Institute for Turkish Policy Studies, ANKAM, *Insight Turkey*, 8, 2, 2006: 7 – 18.

Troll S.J. Chr. (2001*), "Muslime in Deutschland. Ziele, Strömungen, Ogranisationen/Strukturen"   http://www.jesuiten.org/aktuell/jubilaeum/files/   jahre sthema_2001_troll_1.pdf*

United Kingdom Foreign and Commonwealth Office (2004), *"Draft Report on Young Muslims and Extremism"*. UK Foreign and Commonwealth Office/Home Office, available at: *http://www.globalsecurity.org/security/library/report/2004/muslimext-uk.htm*

United Nations (2005) *'United Nations Human Development Report'*. New York and Oxford: Oxford University Press.

United Nations Department of Economic and Social Affairs (2004), *'World Economic and Social Survey 2004. International Migration'* New York: United Nations. Available at: *http://www.un.org/esa/policy/wess/wess2004files/part2web/part2web.pdf*

Warner C. M. and Wenner M. W. (2002), *'Organizing Islam for Politics in Western Europe'*. Hoover Institution, Stanford University, available at *http://faculty.washington .edu/tgill/544%20Warner%20Islam%20Europe.pdf*

Zaidi A. (2006), 'Poverty of Elderly People in EU25' Policy Brief August 2006, European Centre, Vienna, available at:
http://www.euro.centre.org/data/1156245035_36346.pdfsearch=%22Zaidi%20A.%20(20 06)%2C%20%E2%80%98Poverty%20of%20Elderly%20People%20in%20EU25%E2%8 0%99%20Policy%20Brief%20August%202006%2C%20European%20Centre%2C%20V ienna%2C%20available%20at%3A%20%22

Zaidi A. et al. (2006), 'Poverty of Elderly People in EU25. Project financed by the European Commission' available at:
http://www.csmb.unimo.it/adapt/bdoc/2006/41_06/06_41_44_PENSIONI.pdfsearch=%2 2Zaidi%20A.%20(2006)%2C%20%E2%80%98Poverty%20of%20Elderly%20People%2 0in%20EU25%E2%80%99%20Policy%20Brief%20August%202006%2C%20European %20Centre%2C%20Vienna%2C%20available%20at%3A%20%22

INDEX

R

S